Book Four

The Third Prophecy

Second Edition

By K Kobayashi

In this book the author discloses his personal conviction, which, he believes, will decide the people's way of life in one century from now.

Strictly Literary™,
PO Box 242,
Scarborough, Queensland, Australia, 4020.
www.strictlyliterary.com
Phone: 0413 004 138
First published by Strictly Literary, Australia, in 2016

First Published 2016

Second Edition 2020

ISBN: 978-0-9923297-7-8

The author K Kobayashi is issuing the following series of books:

Book One *Idealism and Materialism*
Book Two *Religion*
Book Three *Communism*
Book Four *The Third Prophecy*
Book Five *The Sexual Laws*

Though the series is a coherent unit with the unified purpose, each book is designed to be read independently from the others. The first three books are preparing for the proposal and the last book is augmenting the proposal. His core proposition is in Book Four *The Third Prophecy*; in fact it can be expressed in one simple sentence 'To love a child is not to make one'.

He proposes the love which is the most beautiful and the strongest the humans will ever know; and unless this love is stronger than the love between the sexes the proposal does not make any sense. People imbued with this love gladly discard everything else including their sweethearts. As the concession to an idealised state of being single the sweethearts, unmarried, may remain friends to have sex with precaution against pregnancy. Buddhists and Christians have always taught their adherents to be single all their life. The author firmly believes that marriage has been the greatest curse of the human race. Men and women suffered tremendously through marriage all these millenniums still they could not work out the way out. Only the love of the Third Prophecy leads the ordinary people to stay out of marriage with the unwavering conviction.

This love when adopted by an individual will fulfil what the first (idealism; and religion as crystallisation of idealism) and second (materialism; and communism as an extreme form of materialism) prophecies promised but did not deliver in full to the humans and human societies. This love when adopted by a society as a whole will fulfil not only the first and second prophecies to the full but also will solve many serious problems the humans have had all these millenniums as well as the humans may have in the future. The acceptance of this new way of life by the bulk of the population will result in hugely reduced population with the predominantly beneficial results to the humans. This leaves one serious problem for the ordinary single men and women, that is, how to solve their sexual problem. The author proposes the solution of this problem mainly addressed to single men in Book Five *The Sexual Laws*. He expounds the solution getting the idea from 'mind only' developed by the Buddha; the mind only concept is explained in Book Two *Religion*.

The author wants to prove beyond reasonable doubt that the arrival of the societies dominated by this new way of life is inevitable in the future provided the humans act according to the survival instinct as they have done all these millenniums. Since his message is contrary to the people's way of thinking in the past and present, he thinks that the ordinary people at present do not comprehend the message of the Third Prophecy, and it will take one century for the general public to fully appreciate its teaching and live according to its creed.

Contents

Chapter 1 What is Third Prophecy?

Section 1 Essence

The concept of the Third Prophecy was born in my mind when I was in severe distress in my youth. When people suffer to the extreme, they naturally look for the philosophy, higher or deeper, than the ordinary way of thinking in an effort to escape the painful feeling. I rejected the new thinking for a brief moment once in a while because it entirely went against what I had believed for all my life up to that time. Once the idea formed in my mind firmly, not even for one second have I doubted its correctness. It has grown into a beautiful way of thinking, which, I am sure, will never leave me until I die and my brain decomposes. I am going to expound this philosophy which stands on uncontaminated love and outshines both idealism and materialism at their best. I unwaveringly believe that this concept, though not entirely new to human minds—I learned later, is more beautiful than the most intricate religion and more useful in financial terms than the communist theories put into effect in an idealised society. The benefits of the new way of thinking are due without an exception to both any individual who practise it and any society which embraces it as a dominant ideology, under any religious, economic and political system. The Third Prophecy does not oppose any existing ideologies and stands on its own.

The communistic world view gripped me for several years and departed, and then I became a deeply religious man and the idea of the Third Prophecy was born in my mind, all in my youth. As I grew older and learned many things in life, I have become more and more convinced that the teaching of the Third Prophecy is right even I judge by various criteria and that upon hearing it the intelligent people would choose it as their way of life in addition to the other life views.

Both religion and communism do not fully explain the phenomena of life on its own and at any rate the attempts to impose these ideologies on the world population were largely ephemeral. I do not doubt the sincerity of the protagonists. This small number of people must have wondered why people in general did not respond favourably to their enthusiasm. Confucius confessed before his death that all his teachings on ethics were in vain with all his efforts and sincerities, and did not understand the reasons for failures. In fact people were behaving naturally in this matter and the Third Prophecy justifies the behaviours and I explain the reasons fully as this book is to disclose.

I have found in my life that there are causes for most afflictions such as acquired mental disorders, diseases, wars, family breakdowns and even unhappiness. In many cases people are ignorant as to why certain misfortunes happen to them and are resigned to the notion that these things simply happen or attribute them to the divine intervention.

If readers go through this book, they should be able to understand why the First Prophecy (idealism) and the Second Prophecy (materialism) have been only partially successful. These topics are the subjects of Book One *Idealism and Materialism*. Religion is the realm of the Ultimate and God; idealism is only one way to get to that realm. Communism is the extreme form of materialism, as I understand. I expound these subjects in Book Two *Religion* and Book Three *Communism* respectively. Readers should even recognise that only the Third Prophecy has the real capacity to reform the society and that how stupid people are to preach the previous ideologies under the existing way of thinking. Only after reaching the summit of the new prophecy can people see what the previous generations went through hard and tortuous trails for little gains. The Third Prophecy, which has nothing to do with idealism and materialism in essence, explains why these previous prophecies were not really effective on the lives of the majority of people in spite of the small number of the enthusiasts who were even prepared to sacrifice their lives for their beliefs. If adopted by a large number of people, this new way of life will build a society based on love. This love is not a conventional love and is hard to understand for the ordinary people at this stage of human development, though it is really simple once understood, in a similar manner that many engineering theories looked formidable at my first encounter but were simple once understood. The new prophecy goes against the common belief of the people up to the present and possibly for a century from now; hence I need a great deal of tact to overturn the belief. I devote this book to explaining the nature of true parental love as I have come to know. In its essence, there is only uncontaminated love in the Third Prophecy and readers cannot find anything else in it. To love one's children entails to do what is best for them, disregarding the other considerations such as the welfares of the parents or the nations. In the process I came to the conviction that the parental love in the conventional sense was nothing but the self-love disguised.

A small number of people expressed the core theory of the new philosophy in the course of human history. However, the public at large ignored this insignificant number of people who advocated their faith and lived accordingly. No human society has ever adopted the idea en masse. The reasons for this may lie in the probability that these people could not communicate effectively the bases of their belief or the public were not ready to embrace this new concept of love: both possibilities would have resulted in the same non-action.

The core thinking of this philosophy is well expressed in the sayings of the ancient Greeks in the following passages. When the sage Thales (?624-?546 BC) of Miletus was asked why he was not married, he said, 'I did not want to leave any descendants'. Thales used to say that life and death were matters of indifference. To a man who asked why then he did not die, he replied, 'Because it is a matter of indifference'. (Montaigne 1965, pp. 42, 67) He is sometimes referred to be the founding father of Greek philosophy.

Montaigne also quotes in his *Essays* (begun in 1571) a poem by another Greek philosopher: To love a child is not to make one. Montaigne wrote in another context:

> The commonest and healthiest sort of men considers an abundance of children a great happiness. I and some others regard the lack of them as equally fortunate. (p. 42)

He had six babies, but only one of them lived beyond infancy. He retired in 1571, when he was 38 years of age, to his ancestral home where he was born and devoted his time in writing essays. (p. ix) Montaigne himself, three brothers, and one sister with their parents remained Catholic; however, one brother and two sisters became Protestant. Before he was 30, the religious civil wars had broken out. They continued intermittently all the rest of his life. (p. viii)

Kenko YOSHIDA also expressed his conviction to terminate his issues in his collection of essays, *Tsurezure-gusa* (*Essays in Idleness,* c. 1330). He wrote the above essays during the peaceful shogun (military dictator) rule in Japan, and there was no mention in his essays that he observed a military conflict. He was nominally a Buddhist, and preached the superiority of mind over matter and mocked at the popular materialistic culture. He also called silly of the people who suffered in an effort to acquire fame and wealth. But he was wealthy enough to keep mistresses. He also wrote that all women had warped and perverse minds and he detested these natures of women. He expressed his conviction that people should not leave children in this world whether they were important or not.

All the following authors, Greek and Latin, state only the half of the Third Prophecy in that they mention only the phenomena and do not state how they can achieve this status.

The Greek poet Sophocles wrote:

> It is best of all never to have been born, but second best--second by far--if one has made his appearance in this world, to go back again, as quickly as may be, thither whence he has come (Toynbee et al. 1968, p. 70).

Homer wrote the poem, ' 'T were better far at once to die, than lived hemmed in and straitened thus, in dire distress' (Harbottle 1897, p. 339). Aeschylus read the poem, 'Far better were it once for all to die than one's whole life to suffer pain and grief' (p. 406). He wrote similarly: Death than a life of ill is easier far, and better never to be born at all than live and suffer (p. 383). Cicero taught that by far the happiest fate for a man was not to be born; the next happiest to die very early (p. 172). He wrote, 'The swan, foreseeing how much good there is in death, dies with song and rejoicing' (p. 39). Pliny the Elder wrote, 'Life itself is a punishment, save to the man who has neither sorrows nor ill-health' (p. 165).

The Greek historian Herodotus attributed the same view to the 6th century BC Athenian political reformer Solon. According to Herodotus' story of Solon's conversation with King Croesus, the human beings Solon cited as having been the happiest within his knowledge were not Croesus, as Croesus had hoped, but two young men--a pair of brothers--who had died in their sleep at the height of their strength, achievement and fame, when their mother prayed to the goddess Hera to bestow on them the best lot that a human being can hope for. The comment that Herodotus puts into Solon's mouth is that the brothers 'met with the best possible end that human life can have, and that God took this opportunity for making it manifest that, for a human being, it is better to be dead than to be alive'. (Eliade 1978, p. 260)

Theognis and Pindar similarly proclaimed that the best fate for human beings would be not to be born or, once born, to die as soon as possible (p. 260).

The Bible gives out the following verses:

> Vanity of vanities! All is vanity. (Ecclesiastes 1:2)
>
> And I thought the dead, who have already died, more fortunate than the living, who are still alive; but better than both is the one who has not been, and has not seen the evil deeds that are done under the sun (Ecclesiastes 4:2-3).

Incredibly, the author of Ecclesiastes, probably King Solomon, concludes that life is still worth living, though he does not try to answer the various queries he raised.

Jesus Christ said:

> Truly I tell you, there is no one who has left house or wife or brother or parents or children, for the sake of the kingdom of God, who will not get back very much more in this age, and in the age to come eternal life (Luke 18:29-30).

He further said, 'For the days are surely coming when they say, "Blessed are the barren, and the wombs that never bore, and the breasts that never nursed"' (Luke 23:29). This prophecy matches with the teaching of the Third Prophecy.

During Jesus's ministry he did not show any interest in his mother Mary and brothers and sisters. The fact that the authors do not make any further reference to his father Joseph after the Gospel of Luke--the last reference is in Chapter 3, Luke--makes us suspect that something untoward happened to him: he was dead by this time or left the family from some reason.

The idea not to get married goes against one cardinal teaching of the Old Testament which states that the faithful will have an abundance of descendants.

The Qur'an (the Koran) and *The Thousand and One Nights* give out the following passages:

> Verily Allah has created men into toil and struggle (Qur'an 90.4).
>
> O mystery of birth and death! Why is a man born if he must die? Why live, if death brings forgetfulness of life? But Allah alone understands the purpose of our destiny; it is for us to bow before him in silent obedience. (Mathers 1953, p. 416)

The Buddha was married and had a son before the Enlightenment. After the Enlightenment he did not show any interest in his wife and son. The following passages come from *Rhinoceros Discourse* (Stryk 1982, pp. 220, 222) which the Buddha, according to tradition, preached:

> As a spreading bush of bamboo is entangled in various ways so is the longing for children and wives: not clinging to these, even like a bamboo just sprouting forth, let one walk alone like a rhinoceros.
>
> If one lives in the midst of company, love of amusement and desire arise; strong attachment for children arises; let therefore one who dislikes separation, which must happen sooner or later from those beloved, walk alone like a rhinoceros.
>
> Having abandoned the different kinds of desire, founded on child, wife, father, mother, wealth, corn, relations, let one walk alone like a rhinoceros.

If people are asked what the most important thing is for them, they would most likely reply that it would be their life provided they do not have to show any social courtesy. With a social courtesy, they may say they value their family, friends or even their country most. My answer to the question will be my children beyond comparison with anything else. I feel that all my learning and beliefs are nothing at all in the face of my deep conviction concerning my love to my children. I value my children far more than my own life. If I am further asked what I will do for my children, I will say that I will do what I believe is best for them, that is, I will make sure that I don't have any children of my seed. It is self-evident to me that the best I can do for my children is not to bring them into this world. I am determined not to have any children for their own sake, irrespective of what happens to me who has far less value than my children: it is not important whether I am happy or not, regarding with this matter. Love of the Third Prophecy is beyond the desire for happiness and gains, is pure and stands on its own, not related to anything else in the society, though there are certainly personal and social consequences emanating from its practice. I am also determined not to marry. Since however careful I may be, there is always a chance for my would-be wife to get pregnant. In fact many pregnancies are not planned. Besides my would-be wife may not understand my viewpoint and I have to force my way whether she wants it or not, which is not really a right thing to do. I have become a confirmed bachelor so that I have no chance of leaving my descendants on earth.

Love of the Third Prophecy is stronger than love between the sexes and lasts a life time: otherwise the entire proposal will become nonsensical. If love between the sexes is stronger than love I advocate, the couples in love will marry and have children forgetting the real love for the children. I do not condemn the sexual activities: the believers may engage in love affairs with the precaution against pregnancy but will not marry.

People increasingly use probability and statistics to make a statement, corresponding to the complex and sophisticated society. However, I am absolutely certain without any qualification that by not having children of my seed they will never know what the suffering is and what the death is.

The crux of the teaching lies in loving one's children for the sake of the children and in not having children; it does not preclude having sex with proper precautions. Hence this teaching does not preclude that men go out with women in order to have sex as they do today. I visited many brothels to alleviate my sexual longing with the precautions against having children, venereal disease and AIDS.

'The majority of couples become parent. In North America, for example, only 5 to 7 per cent of marriages in recent decades have remained voluntarily childless. A slightly higher percentages, perhaps 8 to 10 per cent, are childless because the couple is biologically unable to bear children.' (Burnett 1990, p. 854) This is the overall assessment of having children in marriage in North America, and does not state the reasons for being voluntarily childless.

Late marriage, late and fewer children bearing are the characteristics of the American people today (Janus & Janus 1994, p. 225). Many mothers said that being mother was the most gratifying role in their life (p. 216).

According to the Census Bureau, one of every five women in America who are ever married was childless in the 1980s. The reasons for being childless are:

- They dislike children.
- They fear parenthood.
- They are committed to their career.
- They come from dysfunctional family and do not want children to go through hereditary defects which they may pass to children.
- They are biologically unable to have children.

The childless-by-choice is up against the social pressure, especially from their parents (p. 209).

In Australia, 10% of women in 1990 and 25% of women in 2000 do not have any child, not stating both the reasons and whether women are married or not. Further in Australia in 1998, 20% of the married people chose not to have any children, primarily through financial pressure. In 2006 in Australia 37% of all families do not have any children. These data are widely available.

My love towards my kids is absolute and there is no room for compromise. The Third Prophecy flatly disregards the happiness of the parents in favour of that of the unborn babies. That uncompromising attitude is ingrained in me and shows up in my work ethics and in this series of books.

I am to present a couple of stories highlighting the nature of parental love.

According to the Bible, Abraham was so much devoted to God that he was prepared to kill his beloved son without any question when he was asked to sacrifice his son, Isaac, by his wife Sarah, to prove his faith in God (Genesis 22). This degree of belief was astonishing even among the Jews in an era when religion was supposed to reign their life supreme with no other notable ideologies in the overt culture at least. I feel my love in my children is stronger than that of Abraham and I am prepared to sacrifice everything to achieve what is best for my children. Isaac became the father of Jacob who became the patriarch of the 12 Jewish tribes. Isaac was the ancestor of Jesus Christ. The elder son, Ishmael, had been born to Abraham through Hagar, an Egyptian slave girl.

The Parthian Empire exploited the position as a middleman between China in the East and, after the demise of the Seleucids, Rome in the West. The Chinese offered silk and the Parthians, horses; and the first official trade started in 106 BC during the Han dynasty. Parthia was the only state which could match the power of Rome during Augustus' reign. (Freeman 1996, pp. 297, 388)

The following records from the Parthian history are unusual but nonetheless illustrate one man's determination to obtain power even murdering his family. For him the authority of the ruler was more important than the lives of his family.

> Notwithstanding these moves, Orodes in turn was murdered around 40 BC by his own son, Phraates, whom he had already appointed as his successor. Phraates IV (38-32 BC) took preventive measures to ensure that the same fate did not happen to him, executing his

brothers as well as his own son. (Cotterell 1993, p. 165)

My love to my unborn children is an incessant bliss that knows no cease, though it is hard to convey that feeling to readers. If readers get to know the kind of love I am referring to, I am sure that they will be just as determined as I am not to leave any descendants. The ordinary people do not have any problems in carrying out what is required once they recognise the true love towards children according to my definition. Love of the Third Prophecy is the strongest and purest form of love people will ever know through their life. Love I am advocating here is a lot stronger than love between men and women, which is often the subject of the popular novels and movies. Sexual love (sexual act) is certainly strong but this love is a different kettle of fish from the love of the above two kinds: the sexual act is akin to eating and drinking and more a physiological necessity. I deal the sexual problem of single men in Book Five *The Sexual Laws*.

Seneca (c. 4 BC-AD 65), Roman stoic philosopher, wrote, ' 'T is a king's duty to prefer his country to his children' (Harbottle 1897, p. 216). This sentence is in the form of 'ought to' and does not necessarily indicate the reality.

The religious faith can be stronger than love between the sexes. The following is a part of the elegy expressing the friendship between Jonathan and David is deeper than the love of women. David, learning the death of Saul and Jonathan, composed an elegy just before he became king of Judah:

I am distressed for you,
my brother Jonathan;
greatly beloved were you to me;
your love to me was wonderful,
passing the love of women.
(2 Samuel 1:26)

I call feeling towards my unborn babies permanent, human, true and perfect: whereas the common feeling towards born children, impermanent, mammalian, false and imperfect.

The parents have a choice of having children or not for the sake of the parents. But if the focus is on children, the parents don't have a choice, that is, they would not bring the children into this world. Unless the determination to be single all the life comes from love in the way I preach and if it comes from money saving or from perceived happiness--a fair number of people come under these categories, these people most likely will be envious of the married life. Only when the resolution to be unwed is for unselfish love, are the people truly content to be single.

People will naturally ask who would recognise my love to my unborn children apart from myself and also who would carry on the civilisation if my teaching becomes widely practised. My progeny would not feel they are loved by me simply because they are not born into this world. But that is not important to me at all because I have the conviction that I have done what is best for them. My recognition of that belief is sufficient to me. However, this book is intended to let people know the kind of love I am advocating such that people will feel the same love to their own children. Even if this new way of thinking becomes dominant in the society in the next one hundred years or so, there will always be some people who do not agree with it or some people who are not capable of following the teaching from one reason or another. These people will have children and carry on the civilisation, though on a vastly reduced population and on an entirely different premise.

A small number of men through the course of human history did not cohabit with women from the various reasons such as way of life (religious or otherwise), monetary consideration or incapability of acquiring women; however, they were not average people. The average people can live contently not cohabiting with women only if they are convinced with the correctness of the Third Prophecy.

Plutarch (?46-?120) relates the following story in his *Parallel Lives* (c. 100) in relation to the life of Solon (?638-559 BC), an Athenian reformer statesman (North 1967, I; pp. 212-4). Solon was at the house of Thales in Miletus. A traveller mentioned about a funeral of a young man in Athens and Solon eventually got to know from the traveller that the funeral was for his son. Solon beat his head like a mad man with sorrow. Thales, laughing at Solon's anguish, said that the sorrow of this kind keeps him away from marriage and having children. Plutarch as an author inserts his comment that it is wrong not to have honour, goods, knowledge, friendship, virtue, marriage and children, simply because we fear to lose them. It is the human deficiencies to grieve to the extreme over the loss of these objects of affections. People should cultivate themselves not to be over-sorrowful for the adverse happenings of life. It seems that the author misunderstood Thales' idea of not having children. The fear of losing children is only an incidental reason why Thales was not married and did not have children. I say that the fear of losing a child expressed above is a negative approach, though the end result of not having a child is the same as the teaching of the Third Prophecy which focuses solely on love.

There is another example of being single from an unsound concept. Scrooge, the chief character in *Christmas Carol* (1843) by Charles Dickens, did not marry because he loved money so much that he did not want to spend any by setting up his family. Being single based on the new philosophy has the same status as Scrooge did; however, I must stress again that he did not have the fundamental requisite of love towards his children.

The couples may discuss around the time of marriage how many children they like to have. Yet they may have a difficulty in understanding to have zero children. The discovery of the concept of zero was a momentous event in the history of mathematics, though the idea does not give any trouble even to the school children today. In the similar fashion the love of children as I advocate may give some difficulty in understanding today, in the not-too-distant future the people on the street will take the concept for granted.

This world is a strange place to me. Why don't people esteem their children more than they esteem themselves? People work so hard for many years to bring up their progeny, yet they don't seem to know however exhaustingly they labour all their life, they will never come close to what I have done for my unborn offspring.

I have found that the ethical base of the religions the world over may be summarised in 'Love thy neighbour' or 'Love one another' as I expound in Section 3, Chapter 7, Book One *Idealism and Materialism*. It is definitely the universal truth which a few sages formulated in a few parts of the world at the early classical era after many millenniums of agonies and confusions of the human race. People have recognised through the centuries since its discovery that the precept was good theoretically at least but had problems in its practice in the real world. People have not understood why this is so. The answer lies in the teaching of the Third Prophecy. It is impossible for ordinary people to 'Love thy neighbour' before they love their children logically, in terms of strength and practice. It is not logical to expect people who do not love their own children to behave in such a way to love their neighbours who are strangers. I also firmly believe that only when the Third Prophecy makes inroads into consciousness of the ordinary people, do we see the above ordinance in universal and unfailing practice.

To be, or not to be, that is the question-
Whether 'tis nobler in the mind to suffer
The slings and arrows of outrageous fortune,

Or to take arms against a sea of troubles,
And by opposing end them. To die, to sleep-
No more; and by a sleep to say we end
The heart-ache and the thousand natural shocks
That flesh is heir to- 'tis a consummation
Devoutly to be wished. To die, to sleep-
To sleep, perchance to dream. Ay, there's the rub,
For in that sleep of death what dreams may come,
When we have shuffled off this mortal coil,
Must give us pause.

(Shakespeare 1985, 3.1; pp. 56-68)

There are accidentally dreams in a sleep and also a sleep promises us to wake up. Shakespeare did not solve the problem the above soliloquy expressed.

We often hear people say in a dire strait, 'I wish I weren't born'. This feeling, though it may be genuine, does not solve the problem, either.

The Third Prophecy not only answers the above two queries but solves the problem.

The starting point of all Indian philosophy is that we all suffer or life is suffering. The Bible, or I might say the Jewish philosophy, agrees with the above premise. However, the Bible says that the good people suffer for the sake of the good and the evil people suffer for the sake of the evil. It insists that the distinction have the vital difference. It is better, if it is God's will, to suffer for doing good than doing evil (1 Peter 3:17). I have found in my life that many people did not see the difference and chose evil rather than good. Does it really matter in the overall scheme of life how we suffer? Don't we all suffer and die whatever we do or believe?

Both Gautama Siddhartha (the Buddha) and Jesus Christ had the unshakable faith that their ways of thinking were superior to any other thoughts human race had devised and further anyone else in the future would not exceed their state of mind. Christ said, 'Heaven and earth will pass away but my words will not pass away' (Luke 21:33). Also both the ancient to classical Greeks and the Jews all these millenniums, being conscious of distinct bearers of cultures, had the similar conviction and behaved in a rather arrogant manner towards their respective neighbouring peoples.

We can draw the above conclusions easily if we study the utterances of the two religious founders and the history of the two races. The imperial policies to the neighbouring peoples show the sense of cultural superiority by the Greeks: their democratic attitudes were applied only to the Greek men, not to women nor to foreigners; also the general public believed that the slavery was permissible as long as non-Greeks were slaves. The fact that the Jews thought they were superior to the other peoples was clearly shown in the concept of the God's elect and also that the Jewish people should not make their own kind slaves.

Strange thing about the belief in the superiority is that the two individuals and the two races drew the conclusion not by comparing with other thoughts and cultures but solely from their intuition: they simply knew that was the case. These strands of thoughts and cultures developed virtually independently with the exception that the ancient to classical Jews knew much of the Greek culture and wrote the New Testament in Koine or common Greek language, though Christ spoke Aramaic, originally the language of Aram (Syria). Septuagint (the principal Greek version of the Old Testament) was made between the 3rd and 2nd centuries BC, though the Old Testament was originally written in Hebrew language with a few books excepted. The Bible in Greek language spread to the Greek world after the Roman Empire was Christianised in the early fourth century, displacing the Homer's epic poems, *Iliad* and *Odyssey*. Peculiarly enough, I feel the same way about the Third Prophecy and any other philosophy cannot exceed its idea.

The root idea of the new philosophy originated in my suffering. It is hard to describe how much I suffered. Generally it is not possible to convey one's special experience to someone who does not have the similar involvement: the similar exposure conveys the feeling. I cannot state by language or by any other means the deep despair I went through. In its midst I felt the agony my descendants might go through the same suffering and the idea gripped me that they should never experience the same ordeal. Only solution to the horrifying thought was to terminate all my issues. I had the power not to put through my descendants to live through the agony by not bringing them into this world.

Sometimes I wondered why I did not kill myself in order to end the unbearable state of mind and I came up with a few possible explanations. Perhaps I did not have the courage to carry out the killing process. Or I was mentally stronger than I thought I was. Or it was God's will for me to keep living.

My secondary school teacher said in the classroom that his experience as a soldier during the war was so dreadful with many narrow escapes from death that he did not wish any of his children to go through. Even he did not reach to the stage where he wanted to terminate his issues.

'Let the day perish in which I was born, and the night that said, "A man-child is received".' (Job 3:3) Thus Job in the biblical story cursed the day of his birth. Still he did not suffer to the extent to wish that he wanted to terminate his issues such that they would not go through what he had gone through, and subsequently God granted him many descendants.

I firmly believe that only people who go through the unbearable suffering of this world and are strong enough to persevere are capable of understanding the core theories of higher thoughts such as Buddhism, Judaism and the Third Prophecy.

If any human being suffers as much as I did, then that person inevitably does not want to have any children. Only a small number of people among the huge number of the world population hitherto have experienced the despair of that depth. Then am I not wasting this book which tells readers who do not have really agonising life the trial of a tiny portion of human race?

The astute readers would have perceived by now that the message of this book is not to persuade people to follow the Third Prophecy. I have no interest in reforming the society, nor in spreading idealism, nor in improving the economic life of people, nor preventing wars, nor saving humans from extinction, though these consequences may naturally follow if many people practise its teaching. In this book I am revealing my conviction that many people will carry out in the century to come what I believe now. Though most of these people in the future generations would not have agonised to the degree I did, they are on the next and possibly the last evolutionary stage of human development and look at life differently from the ordinary folks of the past and present.

Being single is the best way of life from the viewpoints of Buddhism and Christianity too. Both leaders of these religions taught their adherents to be single to be ideally placed to follow their precepts. In fact, to be single is in accord with the core teachings of these religions. However both religions do not tell the followers how they can obviate their strong sexual desire.

The teaching 'Keep away from marriage' can achieve 'How to become happy'. Happiness is an unimpressive human longing not only in that it is illusive and comes and goes but also in that it is weak in comparison with and often goes against to truth, justice and love. Because of strong attractions between the sexes—sex may be the main among them, people could not adhere to this teaching; however it does not mean people are incapable of achieving this status in the future. No other teachings available to the ordinary people so far have made people live without family with such a firm conviction. Only the arrival of the Third Prophecy will make it possible.

Monasteries (of monks and nuns) in the past and present, and armies and navies (of men) in the past were made up of a single sex. However, the singleness in these institutions was more an incidental status born from the tradition and the necessity. Buddhism and Christianity tolerated marriage, and as far as I could work out the army and navy of the various nations through the history tolerated sex for married and single men while they were in service: the tolerance promoted the effectiveness of the military forces.

Parents-Children Relationships

The babies don't choose to be born into this world but the parents bring them into existence. The children normally find themselves among a group of people such as parents, grandparents

and siblings. Under the usual arrangement, the fathers and mothers give the kids food, clothes and shelter together with affection and protection. The infants, as they grow, learn that nobody other than their parents are to hand over what they need to sustain their life and also come to know that the world around can be quite hostile to them. When faced with certain kinds of problems the children are conditioned to see and consult their parents, who are supposed to give them appropriate advice. So when the parents tell the kids they love them, there is no reasons why the children would believe otherwise.

I clearly remember a short essay written by Somerset Maugham (1874-1965) which I read when I was hardly a man. He was commenting on a tragic case where an adolescent son deserted his parents. The mother said, crying, that they had done everything for their son and even accused him of being ungrateful. However, the author remarked that whatever they did for the youngster, we could not deny the fundamental fact that they brought him into this world for their own sake, ignoring his would-be wish. The young man refused to play the game which the parents wanted him and left them. The parents had certain specifications on their son for them to be happy; they wanted him to behave in a certain way. However, the son did not grow to meet their expectations. The author thought the circumstances under which the desertion took place was not relevant to the issue and hence did not elaborate, thus indicating the general applicability. Certainly Maugham's comment went against the conventional wisdom which would have sympathised with the parents and blamed the young man. It was easy to blame him who was not present to defend himself and besides, after all, the son did not observe the cardinal virtue of honouring his begetters.

The Third Prophecy does not advocate rebellion against parents. In any case I would surmise the theory advanced in this book does not appreciably alter the attitude of people towards their parents even among the supportive readers. It is well established that the personality of an individual is mostly formed during its infancy, especially by three years of age. Seventy-five per cent of brain are developed at birth, and the rest develops in the first five years. I have come to believe that the parent-child relations are not product of accident any more than the fortunes of the bodies such as individuals, firms and nations are not. They all are the results of the thoughts and actions of the people involved as the religions teach us. A careful observer can recognise, as I did on many occasions, how the present status of the existence came about from the past words and decisions. To predict the future is much more difficult since we have the limited knowledge of the entity concerned. It seems that the biblical prophets foresaw the future events from the known circumstances rather than the divine oracles as the Old Testament narrates, and made their thoughts public.

Judging from my experience, how the parents treat the children, especially during their infancy, determines the nature of parent-child relationships. The parents make all the decisions, major as well as minor, within the family when the children are small.

Furthermore, we do not expect, during the years of the offspring' dependency, that the parents' attitudes to their children will change radically; the parents' way of thinking does not alter a great deal over the years under normal circumstances. Thus once set firmly, any amount of theorising obtained from the children' further experiences would not alter their opinions on their fathers and mothers. Looking at the Maugham's essay from this viewpoint, it is the parents who are to blame for the tragedy, even if we forget the proposition that the parents brought the child into this world for their own wellbeing rather than his.

However, after reading this book, many people may look at the parental love in an entirely new light, though they may not change their attitude towards their parents perceptively. They may agree with my proposition that the parental love of the conventional sense is nothing but the parents' selfishness. Some people may even get to the central theme of the Third Prophecy and decide not to have children of their blood.

Racism and sexism are identification or non-identification of the self in the other people. Love is also an identification or resonance between sweethearts. The children are the highest identification of the parents. Friends are also identification among the same or opposite sex. These strong emotions must be innate and ultimately come from the desire for survival.

I am going to cite two examples of the parental love of an ordinary sense, though we can see ample evidence of that in our daily life. I took the first episode from the historical personality. The second story was in the English text, as I remember, at my secondary school and the name of the central character presented is probably not correct. In both cases the characters are self-centred, in all probability not being aware of that fact. Here we can see the seeds of conflicts, individually or socially, in that people are, not realising so, seeking only their welfare, discarding that of others, in these cases, of their progeny.

After the two examples, I expound the relevant thoughts of the historical personalities: Arthur Schopenhauer, Isaiah in the Bible, Bertrand Russel and Socrates. These are not an exhaustive list of the pertinent opinions but are the passages I happened to get to know. It is notable that none of them refer to the love of children as I define.

Jean Jacques Rousseau (1712-78)

He foreshadowed Romanticism, a dominant movement in Europe from the late 1700s to the mid-1800s. Romanticism valued feeling more than reason; impulse and spontaneity more than self-discipline. His spheres of interest were ethics in his youth, and changed to education and politics as he matured.

Rousseau sent all his five children soon after their births to the Paris Foundlings' Home, though he and his mistress, Therese Levasseur, were financially capable of bringing them up at home (Rousseau 1979, p. 17). He had taken up with Levasseur in 1745, an illiterate laundry maid, at the hotel where he was staying. They eventually married in 1768 in a civil ceremony. As a matter of fact disposing children in this way was often done in France at that time. However, his contemporaries severely criticised him of this conduct and made him a social outcast in his late years, though the publications of his books, especially *The Social Contract* (1762) on politics and *Emile* (1762) on education, were the underlying reasons for being rejected socially. He wrote in his *Reveries of the Solitary Walker* (written between 1776 and 1778, and published posthumously in 1782) that he loved his children better than anybody else. He insisted that he was not in a position to bring them up himself, and his wife would have spoiled them. He was well aware that his conduct would make people think that he was an unnatural father and a child-hater. He wrote, 'Any other course of action would almost inevitably bring upon them [his children] a fate a thousand times worse' (pp. 138-40).

Rousseau became a Catholic in 1728 after meeting Madame de Warens. He lost his citizenship of Geneva through this conversion. To regain his citizenship, he reconverted to Protestantism in 1754. *Reveries of the Solitary Walker* says that he was sincerely attached to the religion, and his moral sense had always been a faithful guide to him (pp. 49, 65). He further wrote:

> God is just; his will is that I should suffer, and he knows my innocence. That is what gives me confidence. My heart and my reason cry out that I should not be disappointed. Let men and fate do their worst, we must learn to suffer in silence, everything will find its proper place in the end and sooner or later my turn will come. (p. 45)

In the same book Rousseau wrote an episode which unwittingly reveals to us what kind of a man he was. He attended a dinner at the restaurant, and the elder daughter of the hostess asked him if he had any children. He, unprepared, answered that he did not have any. She smiled maliciously at the company. Rousseau, knowing the stupidity of the answer, thought in his mind a few minutes later that he should have answered her question in a different way. (p. 75) Still he did not disclose his true intent concerning his putting away his children into the orphanage.

His thinking on this matter stands on a false premise. I can tell without any shade of doubt that all his children suffered and died whether they were brought up as orphans or not. Rousseau's judgement could have made some difference, for better or worse, as to how the children agonised through life. Their children might or might not have agreed with his decision, they may change the opinion on this matter over the years, and besides we do not know if the children's opinions are correct or not. In any case, Rousseau's ruling as well as the children's perception is not important in the overall scheme of life, because all his five children suffered and died whatever he did for them.

Rousseau is credited for spreading the concept of social contract and helped shape the political events that led to the French Revolution, thus giving legitimacy to the revolution of the years 1789 to 1799. I am rather suspicious if he deserved the above credit. In the first place I would bet that the revolution would have taken place whether the idea of social contract was in wide circulation or not. Perhaps without it the events might have taken a slightly different course, though we cannot reliably judge if they were for better or for worse. Many contemporary people read Rousseau's *The Social Contract*. For example, Robespierre (1758-94) had a deep faith in what Rousseau wrote. (Wells 1925, p. 569) Robespierre became a French revolutionary and Jacobin leader; he established the Reign of Terror as a member of the Committee of Public Safety (1793-4); he was executed in the coup d'état of Thermidor in 1794. In the second place Rousseau did not invent the notion concerned but expanded and promoted it in the above book. Though the social contract had its root in both Roman and medieval thoughts, Thomas Hobbes and John Locke formulated the idea in a modern setting. Hobbes supported absolute monarchy in *Leviathan* (1651) based on a version of a social contract theory. Locke (1632-1704) bridged the gap between liberty and subordination with a use of the concept borrowed by analogy from commercial practice--the social contract. (Walker 1978, p. 25)

> He [John Locke] thought that society rested upon an implicit contract between sovereign and people, ruler and ruled, and that, when the government broke this understanding the people had the right to change it. The relevance of this to the circumstances of 1688-9 [the Glorious Revolution] was obvious, and it would be appealed to by the American revolutionaries on their way to becoming Founding Fathers of the United States. (Rowse 1979, p. 97)

Mencius (?372-?289 BC) supported the people's right to rebel when the governing body did not do their duties. This political theory is called the Chinese Constitution.

The social contract theory is a most fundamental political thought in modern times but the influence to the French Revolution can be said to be marginal. The testaments in the Bible are the covenants or contracts between God and the followers, whereas the social contract purporting to exist among the people of a community, excluding God in the formula, reflects the unreligious notion in the modern setting. I am not questioning that Rousseau's influence on the modern thinking of the West was immense though his school education was minimal. When he was young he was interested in morals, but as he got older he was more preoccupied with social problems. Ultimately this latter pursuit of his made a big impression on the formation of modern thinking. His moral views remained immature through his life and in his life time he was often criticised for being unethical. His *Confessions* (1782) does not portray him as immoral in his dealings with the other people since he naturally wrote it to justify his existence. As I see him, he did not comprehend the social issues clearly since his thinking did not stand on morals--the fundamental human requirement. His decision to send all his children to orphanage may highlight this point clearly.

> It is this conception of human nature as essentially feeling that forms the basis for all Rousseau's theories. In his *Confessions* he sought to lay bare his soul, proclaiming that at last he would show the world a real man--a picture which certainly contains little of the rational. Rousseau's emphasis on the original feelings and passions of mankind was revolutionary in intent; he wanted to transform social institutions until they conformed to these needs of human nature. (Randall 1976, p. 403)

I shall further cite two more instances which shed some light on his shortcomings of moral and spiritual nature as well as his fundamentally erroneous view about his children in conjunction.

In his old age, he did not understand why people were holding different opinions from those they expressed in their youths. The answer was simple from the religious viewpoint. Rousseau was dealing with the subjects on which people were expected to change opinions. He should have learned from *The Imitation of Christ* (written between 1390 and 1440), which said, 'The old society passes away and the new society arrives, but the teachings of the Lord last forever' (Thomas A Kempis 1952, p. 33), and 'For we more readily turn to God as our inward witness, when men despise us and think no good of us' (p. 39).

After his contemporary society ostracised Rousseau, he wrote in *Reveries of the Solitary Walker*, 'Everything external is henceforth foreign to me. I no longer have any neighbours, fellow-men or brothers in this world. I live here as in some strange planet onto which I have fallen from the one I know' (Rousseau 1979, p. 31). One of the recurrent themes of the Bible is not to be afraid of the human judgements. He would have been a happier man if he had acquired and put into practice the above lesson. If he had been truly a Christian, as he asserted in the previous quotation, the social rejection should not have been hard on him. Or if his conscience had been really clear, he may not have been apprehensive of the hostile opinions of his contemporary people. Or if he had known that the human opinions tend, notoriously, to err and possibly, philosophically speaking, have no inherent value, the disapproval of the other people would have left him unconcerned.

Mrs Cornelia

Mrs Cornelia, a widowed commoner, finding herself surrounded by rich ladies showing off their jewellery, was perturbed for not having any jewels. In the end bringing her son to her side, she said calmly but proudly that he was her precious gem. This episode was quoted such that people should denigrate mammon which was rare and remote but respect mother love which was common and close.

Let me remind readers that the story was told from the viewpoint of the mother nature. Obviously she believed that her child was a treasure which gave her a great deal of joy. However, the anecdote does not answer the query from me and possibly from her son why he had to go through the agonies of life and death, as we all must.

Arthur Schopenhauer (1788-1860)
He was a German often quoted as the philosopher of pessimism. He remained a bachelor all his life. In his works he repeatedly denigrated women, citing that women were not capable of understanding beyond hearing and seeing. Probably he did not marry because he thought that the females were inferior. His father's death in 1805, probably by suicide, was a big blow to him. In 1809 when he came of age, he inherited wealth which was enough to support him the rest of his life. (Janaway 1994, p. 1) In the winter of 1813-4 he was introduced to the Indian philosophy. Later in his life he considered that Upanishad (ancient Hindu philosophy) together with Plato and Kant were the bases of his philosophy. His relationship with his mother became stormy, and in 1814 she threw him out of the home in Weimer for good, and never to see him again. (p. 3) It seems that the cause of the rift was her frivolous way of life which he disapproved. In 1820s Schopenhauer was least productive: He suffered from illness and had an affair with Caroline Richter, a chorus girl at the National Theatre in Berlin. (p. 8)

The Bible
One of the testaments (contracts) between God and his followers is that if the followers keep God's commandments, they will become as numerous as the stars in the heaven and the sands of the seashore.

Isaiah condemns people who criticise the parenthood:

> Woe to you who strive with your Maker,
> earthen vessel with the potter!
> Does the clay say to the one who
> fashioned it, 'What are you making?'
> or 'Your work has no handles?'
> Woe to anyone who says to a father,
> 'What are you getting?'
> or to a woman, 'With what are
> you in labour?'
>
> (Isaiah 45:9-10)

The Bible presents various views on marriage and family. Some passages recommend marriage and some, singleness, though the Bible does not attack the institution of marriage.

Bertrand Russell (1872-1970)
Russell wrote that all the people of today, young and old, male and female, are suffering and further predicted that one thousand years from now, most people would commit suicide. I would say he was wrong on his assessment on suffering of people. I am certain that human beings have had agonising life all their existence since immemorial times, and hence the painful struggle for existence was not confined to his life time as he indicated. His prediction also missed the mark. It is more logical to expect that most people will cease having children before people commit mass suicide.

Socrates (?470-399 BC)
It is well known that Socrates had a dreadful wife, though she bore three sons for him. He kept telling to himself that putting up with his shrew would enhance and strengthen his

personality and hence she was beneficial to him. Socrates, when asked which was preferable, to take or not to take a wife, said, 'Whichever a man does, he will repent it' (Montaigne 1965, p. 647). He would have been probably right under the philosophy he was exposed to, but guided by the new thinking of the Third Prophecy people are glad to remain single all their life as I have been.

Section 2 Various Kinds of Love Compared

The word 'love' in common usage means deep affection or attachment to various objects, animate and inanimate. In some casual situations people use the word 'love' to express mild liking. It can exist between parent and child; God and devotees; sweethearts; and friends. Persons may feel an attachment to authority, ideology, honour, arts, money, drugs, alcohol, gambling and sex; and the aggregate of people such as family, institution, country or race. Upon reflection we notice that some of the above-mentioned love are considerably unlike and some entirely different. It is amazing that the same word denotes such wide spectrum of affections without causing practical problems.

One major characteristic of love except for God is that it exists between the persons and the entities whose possession, use, contact or wellbeing they hold dear. The affection thus generated may not be reciprocal, as we often hear of jilted lovers or deserted parents. In any case love is not reciprocal when the objects are inanimate. In all the above examples except for God, the absence of the object would cause severe anguish in the loving individual. *The Dhammapada,* a Buddhist canon, teaches that we should not meet loved ones nor unloved ones since it is suffering not to meet loved ones and also suffering to meet unloved ones (Narada 1993, p. 181). A concept of God cannot be forcibly removed unless the individual so wills. Judging from this perspective, God as an object of adoration is superior to the other objects. The authors of the Bible and the Qur'an (Koran) repeatedly remind readers of the transitory nature of the worldly pursuits such as mentioned above in the hope that they will leave the vulgar attachments behind. The Bible says: Because we look not at what can be seen but at what cannot be seen; for what can be seen is temporary, but what cannot be seen is eternal (2 Corinthians 4:18). It also says: Now these three remain: faith, hope and love. But the greatest of these is love. (1 Corinthians 13:13) The joys derived from the worldly passions are, the Bible and the Qur'an teach, temporal and always accompanied by fear and anguish. The happiness derived from the vulgar pursuits is the worldly happiness, low and temporal, and different from the spiritual happiness, high and permanent, as the various religions teach.

Mistakes are inherent in decision makings. Howard Hughes, an American industrialist, film producer and aviator, had a personal rule not to make a decision, and let other people do such that he could blame the person who made the wrong decision. We may further argue that it is a mistake to be attached to the worldly enjoyments, which always bring sooner or later, in some way or another, some anguish and unhappiness, though we do not deny that they give us temporal happiness or pleasure. The sense of happiness or pleasure, though temporal, is the reason why the persons seek such vulgar passions as drug taking, alcohol drinking, gambling, sex, tobacco smoking, money making, fame seeking, power grabbing and child rearing. They are all different and many people do not comprehend why other people are attached to some of the above pursuits; however, majority of people are addicted to money making and sex. For the love of money is a root of all kinds of evil, and in their eagerness to be rich some have wandered away from the faith and pierced themselves with many pains (1 Timothy 6:9-10). Love of God and love of children as I define are beyond any sense perceptions and do not produce any unhappiness per se hence are superior to any other pursuits in this sense also.

The love I am advocating in the Third Prophecy is similar to the love of God in this light. Unborn children are akin to God; both are beyond our senses and can be objects of adoration; both concepts are beyond all living creatures except by human beings. Only those men and women with well-developed intellect are capable of cognising the unseen entities such as God or unborn babies. Nobody can deprive me of my love towards my unseen babies and I have absolutely no fear of losing them. I am perpetually submerged in a bliss, though that fact is not on my conscious mind when I am thinking about the subjects at hand. There is no exertion required to maintain the status quo. I had to go through denial periods when the adjustment must have taken place at the initial stage of conversion until the theory firmly got hold of me.

Both love of God and love of children in my definition are hard to visualise; however, the former is expressed as obedience to the God's precepts (1 John 5:3) and the latter as not having children, in a concrete form. Christ said: Whoever has my commands and obeys them, he is the one who loves me (John 14:21). As a matter of fact love of God entails more than the above concrete expression since many peoples in the world over discovered the moral disciplines which are similar to the God's ordinances of the Bible. Likewise, love of children encompasses wider and deeper thought than the above concrete manifestation since not having children may be incidental results of such as biological defects, economic pressure or anticipated emotional burden in raising up children.

Love of children as I define is analogous to the enlightenment some Bodhisattvas experienced: they suddenly understood what they brooded over and suffered about for many years, and after some adjustment periods felt the conceived idea would never be lost.

Enlightenment may be defined to be a state beyond all suffering (Lopez 1987, p. 17). In fact an enlightenment happens in a much less dramatic and non-religious context. Suddenly the answer to a puzzle dawns on us, whether it be about a casual remark by somebody or over a mathematical problem. The realisations stay with us for the rest of our life. There is a good example of enlightenment from the Christian tradition. St Augustine agonised himself wondering why the selfish people could live without suffering and he eventually obtained the answer and ceased agonising over the topic. Jeremiah expresses the same anguish in the Bible: Why does the way of the wicked prosper? Why do all the faithless live at ease? (Jeremiah 12:1)

I have written this book in the hope of passing my enlightenment and love thus conceived to the general public. We can convey knowledge and wisdom with words but cannot fully express love in language. Many popular movies try to tell what sort of love the young sweethearts have for each other through the plots. The Bible teaches us to love the fellow human beings and God, using various means; history, poems, utterances of the prophets, knowing fully well that written words cannot impart love directly.

Love between Men and Women

The love towards the unborn babies I am advocating should be stronger than the love between the sweethearts. Some people I knew well to whom I confided that I had deserted my sweetheart reacted vigorously, saying that I was cruel, she might still keep loving me and I was the one who had to take the initiative and so forth. They all misunderstood me since I did not explain the thinking behind the desertion. Even if I had taken a few minutes to tell why I made the decision of separation, they could not have assessed the notion correctly. It takes a book such as this to get to the bottom of the matter.

I met my love when we were 16 years of age and we fell desperately in love the following year. I loved her as much as any man possibly could love a woman and she reciprocated it with the similar affection. The strong emotion lasted till I went back to the university at the age of 26. I hardly think about her now, approaching an old age. I have absolutely no regret for the fact I left her. Though my attachment was as intense and genuine as could be between the couple in acute love, that was nothing at all compared with my affection to my children I hope I would never see. I hope that readers may get some insight into the depth of my love for my unborn babies.

During the period while I was in love, my sexual desire persisted and I wanted to make love to every good-looking girl. I now believe that love between the sexes and the sexual desire are two different things. The love towards the sweetheart is in a sense false in that a man loses an interest in his sweetheart after so many lovemaking sessions in the ordinary course of events and the man does not mind having sex with any other good-looking woman even before losing an interest in the sweetheart.

Section 3 Two Kinds of Parental Love Contrasted

It is hard to convey to readers my burning love towards my unborn offspring. I am going to attempt just that in this section by one way available to me: contrasting it with the parental love of conventional sense.

Impermanent vs Permanent

I am perpetually submerged in a blissful love, and I can recall that love to my unborn children whenever I direct my mind to it. I have never doubted the correctness of my belief--not even for one second--once the idea firmly rooted in me. If any parent of the ordinary sense has a doubt, for whatever brief moment it may last, as to bringing the child into this world, for whatever reasons it may be--from nursing or from the suffering of the child, then they lose against me in terms of duration.

A married man with a few children told me that he regretted marrying at some stage in the past but he was happy about his married life in the overall assessment. He did not realise that he lost against me because I did not regret being single not even for one second.

Mammalian vs Human

Most people identify their offspring with themselves as undoubtedly mammals do; both of these warm blooded animals see themselves in their issues. Humans and mammals belong to the same animals of a class: humans are mammals. However, under the above heading I am to contrast mammals excluding humans with humans here.

The mammalian and human parents love their children, thinking their offspring are the parts and the other selves. They believe that this affection is a natural and immutable truth. They do not question any further: In fact they cannot because the brain structures of mammals and ordinary humans are not well developed to go deeper than what nature ordained as far as the parental love goes. I wrote this book in order to change the perception of the humans in this respect. Both normally do not look at their children as something of a burden which they are obliged to bring up. We often witness the intensity of mammalian and human love of their offspring in the course of our daily life.

This love does not come about by accident. We can see a train of strong feelings originating in strong sexual desire of mammalian males as well as of human males. The highly charged lust of males manifests itself in fierce competition to acquire females and consequent intensive lovemaking, which in due course leads to strong parental attachment to their children. Because of these trains of the intensities, people don't doubt that these mammalian and human behaviours are genuine and natural.

The seemingly strong attachment by parents to their offspring is, from another angle, an instinct to preserve a small number of children thus produced. Low forms of life, such as plants and fish, do not have such an attachment to their offspring not only because they do not have well-developed thinking faculty but because they produce a huge number of offspring. By the similar logic, I would imagine a king with a large harem and a large number of children possibly do not have a strong emotional tie to his issues. And the above tendency accelerates by the heavy responsibility of governing as well as by the various entertainments available to the potentate.

Each parent, mammalian or human, has different sort of love towards his or her offspring, each being different identity with differing personality and outlook, though it may be all collectively called parental love. The parental love is certainly different from the love between sweethearts. The English language and possibly any other language do not differentiate these two forms of love. Every sweetheart has, again, different kind of love. It is commonly believed that the parental love is so intense that the parents are often at a loss how to express this feeling to other people including their children.

Interestingly enough, both mammals and humans on rare occasions reject the newly-born babies and do not want to have anything to do with them from some unknown reasons. This fact illuminates one deficiency of parental love in the customary sense of the phrase. Occasionally it is reported in the media that a mother might have killed her baby. I imagine in some cases the mutual dislike developed whatever she did for her baby; in some cases she did not want to bother to bring up the baby. In all cases she does not admit she murdered the baby despite the strong evidence she did, and does not disclose the reason. ET Seton in his book *Wild Animals I Have Known* (1898) does not record an instance where an animal rejects its offspring in his multitudes of stories. Probably he witnessed a few instances of rejection but he did not want to record them, most likely thinking the behaviour was out of the character for the animals he loved observing.

Mammals can never feel anything towards which they cannot see such as God or non-existent children. Mammals can never have any emotional attachment to unborn offspring. Similarly it is hard for me to imagine people on the street today experience the affection at the imaginary level. Only a tiny proportion among highly intelligent people through human history have felt love towards the non-existent children and consequently abstained from having any. Only people in general at the next evolutionary stage can love children which do not exist. Mammals are not capable of understanding and practising the concepts of 'Love thy neighbour', neither materialism, nor the Third Prophecy: they are capable only to behave as their instincts dictate and to love their offspring in the flesh.

False vs True

My decision not to have children solely comes from the perceived welfare of my children, that is, on what is best for them. The people of the world make progeny for the perceived gains for the parents such as biological, financial, emotional, cultural; though many of them do not believe or admit that is the case. Many parents told me that their children gave the joy to live and also having children is the happiest experience in their life. Karl Marx came to believe that surplus value was equal to multiples of the aggregate wages of the employees; the parents all over the world came to believe that they loved their children. Both beliefs resulted from repeating the sentences many times over the years since the idea suited both Marx and the parents, though both notions originated in false premises.

Whatever the motives for parenting, once the parents have a family of their own, they are busy in carrying on the business of supporting it. They don't want to be bothered with the reasons or motives behind the scheme since the theorisation of this nature does not help them in their daily life.

Euripides read a poem: The sweetest thing, my child, the bitterest too (Harbottle 1897, p. 321). This verse indicates that the joy accompanying parenting is coupled with fear. Thus having children has fatal flaws as expected from its selfish but covered-up motives. The parents are afraid that their kids may injure themselves, desert them, or die. This is another manifestation of deficiency in the parental love of ordinary kind. What the parents want to believe to be love is of flesh and of lower order, and in fact is not love at all compared with higher and spiritual love of which I am advocating in this book. Consequently the parents of this world are beset with the accompanying distresses.

I still clearly remember a conversation I had with a father of five children. He admitted that the family life got too much for him on occasions and he felt like leaving his family behind and living on his own on the remotest place from them, not caring about them.

This kind of feeling happens to average fathers but the relatively small number of them carry it out in the real life. On rare occasions the fathers kill their family and at times even themselves. The main thrust of the argument in this book proceeds on the feeling of the average fathers and not on the small number of the fathers who desert or murder.

It is interesting to note that people who become parents for their perceived welfare suffer as a rule than people who do not have a child for its own sake. The effort to love their children as I define is infinitely less than that to bring up their children. It seems to me that the above phenomenon is more in accord with the laws of happiness which may come under the general principles of the religious law or the cosmic law, though the pursuits of the latter laws lead not necessarily to happiness of mankind but always to justice, virtue and beauty. Idealism is in the realm of 'ought to'. Not many idealist teachers of the world emphasised 'Love your children' since they believed that people practised this concept universally. The following verse is the only exception I have found: Then they can train the young women to love their husbands and children (Titus 2:4). Little did these teachers suspect that the emotion which they took for granted was in fact erroneous and the fundamental cause of the problems which people were having in their daily life and whose solution the sages were striving for.

<u>Imperfect vs Perfect</u>

Rarely can we use the word 'perfect' to describe any action or status but the term is fitting to express my love towards my unborn babies. I am the sole judge not to have children; nothing can enter into that resolution. Whereas if people have children, there will always some probability that the children may rebel and deny the very parenthood of the progenitors as we sometimes witness in the course of life. They don't necessarily express it in a verbal assault in a direct manner. They may behave in a way the parents find unacceptable; desert the parents or even commit suicide. I cannot think of any effective defence the parents can put up if their children thus challenge them. The normal reactions of the parents are they love and care for them and often blame the peer pressures or the society for the tragedy. I am stressing here that the love the parents are referring to is not perfect and in fact a self-love disguised.

To be absolutely fair to the children, people must have permission to bring them into this world. This is of course impossible in practice. The parents use their judgement, whether it is right or wrong and whether the children concur or not. I would say the parents start the family for the preservation of the species and with the pretence of love.

In conjunction with Judaism and Buddhism, I contrast the concepts of relative truth and absolute truth. Chapters 2 and 3 of Book Two *Religion* refer. Here I would say that the parental love of the ordinary kind is relative truth and that of my definition is absolute truth. There is an infinite difference between the two truths as I present. I expound that the essence of both Judaism and Buddhism does not lie in ethics or in the practice of 'Love thy neighbour' but in love of God for the former and in Mind Only (or Emptiness) for the latter. In both religions the higher order negates the lower order. In the similar fashion the love of children in the higher order as I advocate negates the love of children in the flesh--the lower order.

Section 4 Three Typical Questions

When I told people that I did not intend to marry all my life, some did not take the remark seriously in the absence of any underlying explanations. Among the others who believed me, the typical reactions were a mild surprise followed by these questions:

a Don't I feel lonely?
b Who will support me when I get sick or old?
c How do I get sex?

Shopping, cooking, washing the clothes and linens, and maintaining the property were so trifle that nobody bothered to ask me about them.

I probably spend 6 hours a week for shopping, cooking and laundering. I also use up roughly 3 hours every week to clean and maintain the garden and the house. These allotted times are for what we call chores of everyday life and do not include any special work which I carry out from time to time. The time used for all chores as estimated above is less than 10 hours a week; there are 168 hours in one week.

Reply to Question a

In my life as a bachelor I felt lonely occasionally from some reason or another such as I had to part with my sweetheart or I had a learning difficulty at university. However, on the whole I believe that the degree of loneliness I went through living alone was less than the average people with the family. People must understand that the depressing thought of being abandoned is not mere bodily isolation but a mental attitude.

I knew a self-defence expert who used to tell me that he was afraid of isolation, though he was married with a few kids. He also said that he was half regretted about marriage. He should have known that being alone and feeling lonely were two unrelated sets of human conditions. Further he was undoubtedly not aware and I myself was not at the time that he could have overcome the problem by proper guidance and practice. He should have gone through the counselling to reduce the fear of being alone, rather than spending so much time in practising self-defence.

Bertrand Russell taught young people that they should train themselves such that they were not afraid of being alone. Similarly, Arthur Schopenhauer wrote that relying on friends or families to try to avoid loneliness was a sign of mental shortcoming: Mature men should face and overcome the lonely feeling on their own.

Reply to Question b

This concern is laughable for anyone who cherishes unborn babies above anything else in the world. However, I may best answer the question in the following fashion.

Death Bed. The worst scenario I may possibly end up may be conjured up in the following way. I get really sick one day and I find unable to lift myself for lack of strength. I cannot get to the telephone, nor feed myself, nor answer the call of nature. I realise, lying in my filth, that I am going to die in a few days.

This story line does not worry me at all. I cannot see why dying in the hospital surrounded by my family is any better. I would imagine that the sense of happiness coming from children at the departing time will be cancelled by the sadness of separation. Hence, even judged from the purely emotional viewpoint, I don't see any sense when some parents say that they brought up their children so that they may not die alone. In the nursing bed I may be well looked after and live a bit longer with a few injections. I may be even cured of the illness which started the problem in the first place.

If, put in the above situation, I regret what I did concerning my children, I should not be writing this book. I will die in the firm belief that I loved my children in the best and only way I could.

A Conversation. A Frenchman and I worked with the other fellow workers as maintenance mechanics on the same floor. Our job was to get the machines going when they broke down. Since our service was required only when a machine malfunctioned, we sometimes had time to converse on a topic. One day we started talking about the family. He was married with a few children.

When I said that I had no family and did not intend to get married, he said quickly, possibly as a response to what he did not expect to hear, 'If you get sick, who will look after you?'

I said, 'It does not worry me at all. I can take care of myself if the sickness is minor. I am prepared to die if I get seriously ill. What if you become sick, minor or major? Are you not more concerned than I am because you have the responsibility to support your family?'

He replied self-assuredly, 'You are right. Married men would be more worried'.

Reply to Question c

This question about sex is legitimate. Being single and excessively introverted, I was beset with the serious sexual problem. Though many girls showed an interest in me while I was young, I was unable to carry out what I really wanted, that is, to go out and go to bed with them because I was extremely shy. Another problem was that I did not know that the sexual matters had certain laws I had to comply with. I explore these laws in Book Five *The Sexual Laws*. Apart from getting acquainted with the laws concerning sexual activities, aging has helped me alleviate the difficulty and at this time I would say that sex is not a serious problem anymore.

Section 5 Marriage as Institution

The families have existed all over the world at any stage in human existence, though the forms of the families varied a great deal. For the social anthropologists it is the principal area of research to look into the reasons for the universality and diversity of its manifestations. (Burguiere et al. 1996, p. 9) A wide variety of family configurations can be identified. The essential form may be nuclear family and many forms of extended families, and that of group marriage.

The family is a natural phenomenon like language and an attribute of the human condition (p. 10).

Prohibition on incest was known in all cultures and was universally associated with the practice to marry outside the narrow circle of kinship. Thus the taboo of incest became the means of forging alliance between the different groups of kinship. Marriage was an opportunity to create new economic and social relationship. (p. 27) The girls were exchanged for gifts. The transition from nature to the above culture came out universally. (p. 12)

There is no direct evidence concerning pre-historic attitudes towards sex and family. Archaeological data indicate the existence of family units. Anthropological data obtained from primitive cultures in modern times suggest some sexual practices. Probably there were a wide variations and taboos in the sexual practices of prehistoric people. (Lloyd 1964, p. 443)

The existence of families is closely tied to the existence of a society. There would be no society without families and there would be no families if a society did not already exist. The family emerged at some point in time that will remain forever a mystery. (Burguiere et al. 1996, p. 65)

The family exists not only for the fulfilment of sexual obligation but the consideration of an economic nature. Some researchers concluded that sex was the prime factor for the establishment of marriage and some, economic consideration. In fact both considerations are in marriage. Marriage may be a unit to solve sexual desire or a better economic unit for the family with children. Sex plays the major role in deciding to get married and after having children the economic factor plays the major role. Men want both to monopolise women as sexual objects and to have the assurance that the children thus born are theirs and nobody else's. Marriage also lays the foundation for a sexual division of labour which has the effect of making both sexes dependent on each other: cooperation is necessary in order for the marriage to survive. (p. 66) The division of labour binds the family together, with neither spouse able to do without the other (p. 80). These observed rules do not extend to the group marriage.

The prehistory, that is, before the writing was introduced into the human society, represents more than 99% of human life on earth. During the prehistory, stretching hundreds of thousands of years, the family and the family relation were formed. (p. 71) The anthropologists know very little about the family at the time of the hunters and gatherers or the first peasants (p. 83). The artefacts and the remains of the bodies in the burial grounds before the writing give some clues if the group was endogamous or exogamous (p. 85).

Of the 90 species of primates there is not a single species in which females exercise authority within the group. However, among the European deer and bison we find the group which females lead. A prehistoric human group was small, comprising a few dozen individuals at most. All social mammals living in small groups are in the habit of exchanging progenitors. Deer and lions do so in a systematic fashion. The migration of the young males and females is essential for the survival of the species. (p. 76)

The exchange of young human males and females between groups has an advantage of enlarging the genetic pool, and avoids the incestuous marriage. We don't know how it was done but are certain it was carried out according to the strict rules established during the prehistoric period. (p. 77)

The two greatest religions of the world, Buddhism and Christianity, regard celibacy as most desirable for the adherents. However, seeing the difficulty of refraining from sex for most men, both doctrines are tolerant of marriage for the lay followers as well as for the denominated except for the Catholic Church's prohibition of marriage on the priests. The authority of these religions is not against the institution of marriage as such but they want the devotees to be single such that they can concentrate on learning their way rather than on the worldly affairs. Married people are obviously constrained financially and also in terms of time, and will be criticised if they neglect their family and devote too much time and effort to the spiritual matters.

Contrary to the general tolerant attitude, there has been a tradition in Christian faith to do without marriage:

> The struggle to impose celibacy on the clergy persisted for centuries and was only moderately successful until well into the Middle Ages. The psychological drives that motivated the imposition of celibacy and the reactions evoked by the assumption of incompatibility of sexuality and spirituality were of tremendous force. (Lloyd 1964, p. 448)

Judaic tradition, that is, Judaism, Christianity and Islam, does not oppose the social institutions such as family and slavery, ruler and ruled relation and social hierarchy, whereas Buddhism does not have the social message, that is, it neither approves nor disapproves them. 'Introduction to Series', Book One, explains why I include Islam in Judaic tradition.

The Old Testament takes the marriage for granted as the following passages indicate;

> Enjoy life with your wife whom you love, all the days of this meaningless life that God has given you under the sun—all your meaningless days (Ecclesiastes 9:9).
>
> Two are better than one, because they have a good return for their work: If one falls down, his friend can help him up. But pity the man who falls down and has no one to help him up. Also, if two lie down together, they will keep them warm. But how can one keep warm alone? Though one may be overpowered, two can defend themselves. (Ecclesiastes 4:9-12)

It says it is warm if two lie down together. That may be true during winter but during summer it is too hot. Also most of the other passages in the above quotes are contrary to my experience as a single man.

Under the Roman law, slaves could not marry but entered into the cohabitation arrangement, resulting in having children. The owners condoned these 'family' arrangements, preferring slaves who had been born into slavery to those bought in the markets. (Freeman 1996, p. 457) Surplus slaves could be sold for profit in the same way with surplus cattle.

First Lateran Council (ninth ecumenical council) of the year 1123 condemned simony and clerical marriage. Lateran Council is any of the five ecumenical councils of the Roman Catholic Church held in the Lateran Palace in Rome.

'Do not commit adultery' is an important precept of both Buddhism and Judaism. This teaching prohibits not only such observable deeds as masturbation and sexual intercourse but also sexual thought. Jesus Christ said, 'Every man who looks at a woman with lust has already committed adultery with her in his heart' (Matthew 5:28). However hard I have tried over many years, I have not been able to stop this adulterous habit. Even if I had been married, possibly I would not have given up this bad habit. Married men may not be able to remove their sexual inclination to beautiful women but average married men should be able to control themselves such that they do not commit sexual impropriety outside marriage.

I said to a few people present at work, 'If people know before marriage precisely what they are getting into--financial and various other problems, the average people would not marry'. One of them, who was probably married, made an emphatic remark, 'If people know precisely what they are getting into, nobody would marry'.

Happy marriages are the exceptions to the general rule of unhappy marriages, and form at least a minority within a community.

I said to a married man when we heard somebody in the next room talking about marriage, 'In all the human activities, marriage is the worst thing you can do. Whatever you do; you rob a bank or kill a person, don't get married'. He said, 'I agree with you. I learned the hard way'. Sure enough, he got a divorce a few years later paying a high divorce settlement fee.

The precise forecast on the individual case is impossible, but we can more or less predict what the average marriages would be like studying the statistical evidence out of the large number of marriages. I am sure it would come out negative in each scale of happiness and finance. In spite of the above prediction of poor pictures of marriage, many people still marry believing that they are not average and can do better, and their partners are special. As a matter of fact, it is established that one half of marriages in 2002 in Australia ended up in divorce. It is also estimated that two-thirds of marriages in 2004 in Australia ended in divorce.

Van de Velde writes in *Ideal Marriage* (c. 1926) that he could not stop his marriage becoming unhappy after the short honeymoon. He continues. There is no doubt that marriage is often a failure and much is suffered in and through marriage. (Velde 1965, p. 3) In the above book he stresses that since sex is the foundation of marriage the unhappy marriage can be turned around to ideal marriage by improving the sex life scientifically: he believes that marriage is a science. Another effective way of preventing the constant perils of mental and psychic alienation in marriage may be to have mutual interest in something, for example, jobs, games or children. (p. 6)

Van de Velde asserts that marriage is:

- sacred to the believing Christians,
- indispensable to the social order,
- absolutely necessary in the interests of children.

(p. 3)

He further writes. There is a perpetual combat between instinctive sexual attraction and equally instinctive sexual repulsion. By scientifically studying the two forces, the attraction can be the permanent stay, suppressing the repulsion. (p. 13)

It is reported that even Albert Einstein (1879-1955) with all his brilliant brain in physics had serious marital problems. He married twice. The first marriage ended in a divorce though his wife was a physicist. The second marriage ended in the death of his wife, his first cousin.

The number of people who is competent enough to participate in the Olympic Games is small, and the number of the winners among them is really small indeed. However, this small chance of winning is not a deterrent to make an effort, rather is esteemed as a high honour. Similarly, the number of happy marriages is small but it seems this does not prevent people getting married and trying hard.

Marriage goes against happiness and acquisition of wealth for most men. We do not have to carry out the survey to establish that happy marriages are rare. Also we do not have to rely on the economists that the average men are better off financially to be single than to be married. Still the majority of men opt for marriage seemingly because of men's strong sexual desire for women. Stated negatively, many people, dreading the loneliness more than the fear of bondage, get married (Smith 1968, p. 116). Marriage and creating the family have been up to the present and will be probably a century from now the means of survival within the society. Until the arrival of the new philosophy of the Third Prophecy most men cannot refrain from marriage.

The mass media often report bashings and murders. I am certain the domestic violence even among socially eminent people has been the serious problem for all these centuries but has not become the social issue until recently. Also among all the murders committed in Australia nearly half are committed by the members of the family. All these observations say that the family life has many serious problems.

Transition from singleness to marriage is easy. Transition from marriage to singleness is harder because money and emotion are entangled intricately; the divorce is lots harder if children are involved. I believe that their children are the main reason why many married couples stay together in spite of the difficult life.

When Europe made the colonial expansion into the world in the 18th and 19th centuries, many European nations did not make money from the possessions of colonies. The notable exception was Britain which derived wealth out of the colonies. Many nations kept the colonies with financial losses. We can see the similar pattern concerning marriage. Most men lose money maintaining their wives still they hang onto them. One of the reasons is undoubtedly the pride in the possessions of both the colony and wife. People are proud to show their possessions and have some prestige in mixing with the other nations in case of colony and their friends in case of wife.

The firms and government want the people under their care to have families even today. In the feudal societies in Europe, and especially in China, the families were the focal points of control. These societies were organised around the families. When a member of the family misbehaved, the rest of the family received the criticism if not the punishment. Therefore the family members had to keep an eye on the conducts of the other members. Marriage was often the affairs of the families rather than the individual members as it is today.

The awful reality of marriage and family life are not surprising in the light of the Third Prophecy, which states that marriage and family are created on erroneous premises and hence it is natural that there are too many problems in maintaining them. It stands for reason that the people who do not love their children as I define get into matrimony captivated by the opposite sex, and suffer as a consequence. To live alone has been a fulfilling experience for me all these years with the set purpose that I have done what was best for my children.

It is not that I have not seen good marriages at first hand but they were few and far between. The good marriages I witnessed were more accidents rather than makings of the couples involved. Bertrand Russell commented that if the couples do not expect happiness prior to marriage, they have a fairly high chance of having happy marriage. He also believed that good sex life has a great deal to contribute to happy marriage. The former has a logical base in that high expectation leads to disappointment, quarrel and unhappiness. The latter belief also makes a good sense since the humans and possibly any other living things are remarkably adaptable creatures. If their spouses are sexually of a great use, they tend to forget the various shortcomings of the spouses. The sense of sexual usefulness on the subconscious level gives rise to the emotional tolerance at the subconscious level. They don't think in the logical sequence that since the spouses are sexually useful they can put up with something else. Everything is done subconsciously.

People today and through the human history have not spared much thought as to the reasons why a man and a woman live together leaving their respective parents behind, in spite of the enormous resources and efforts required to keep the marriage together. The marriage institution suited men and women alike from their intuitive and possibly selfish viewpoints, though they sacrificed happiness and finance as a result.

A huge number of scholars have put enormous efforts to work out the productive and commercial environments; however, only a little effort was put into the workings of the family, though even the full-time workers spend more time in the family than in the firms. I have come to the conclusion that the family organisation is just as complex as that of the productive and commercial organisations, if we focus our attention to the dealings of one person. Certainly a large number of people with different functions are involved in a large firm; hence its organisation is far more complicated than a single family.

Marriage is a way of life, a custom, a convention and a culture that have survived through the millenniums: the rise and fall of civilisations, migrations and wars. People accept its existence as a matter of course. This fact makes us presume that marriage is a form of survival. Children are brought up to believe that it is natural and proper to marry when they reach a certain age. As they grow they see their friends tie their knots around with pomp and ceremony with many happy faces, and they do not doubt when the time for them arrives. They believe that with friendship or love the cohabitation will work, though the reality goes against the assertion for the majority of them.

People are told time and time again since they are babies that all good people are to marry, though the reasons are not clearly specified. The parents, the school teachers and the government authorities all talk to the children as if marriage is an eternal and unalterable truth and proceed any discussion from that premise. The general public get the impression that people who preach non-marriage for the happier and wealthier life are like people who preach revolutionary social reforms: both are misguided and will be disappointed in the end. As a consequence the children are brought up to reject any other notions. Interestingly enough, many young men, both before and after the puberty, form negative opinions about marriage, getting the idea from the abundant unsuccessful marriages around. They quite often express their wish to live without wives. However, in due course the social convention and possibly the sexual drive overpower them into matrimony. Young men decide to get married thinking their fiancés are special and they can lead good life together, though in terms of the probability they are wrong. If people think that their marriage will be similar to that of their parents--monotonous, burdensome, full of quarrels and financial problems, not many people would marry.

People do not question why they marry, but spend a lot of time thinking whom they should marry and how they should proceed with marriage. The ancients carried out many religious rituals such as animal and human sacrifices, not questioning why but paying attention only how they did. Similarly the kids today do certain daily rituals not knowing why they do but simply because they are told to do by adults.

Many men expressed their negative opinions about their wife and marriage through history, getting the ideas from their own experience.

The ancient to classical Greek thinkers presented the following passages. Menander wrote, ‘Without care thou'lt live thy life unmarried’ (Harbottle 1897, p. 321). The same author wrote, ‘Fair will thy life be if thou art unwed’ (p. 339) in another context, resulting in an emphasis. ‘Marriage is full of care.’ [Theocritus] (p. 342) ‘Once you are wed, no longer canst thou be Lord of thyself.’ [Alexis] (p. 372) ‘If you are late, your wife assumes you're having an affair with someone, or someone with you, drinking, banishing care; that you alone have all the fun, she all the ills to bear.’ [Terence] (Montaigne 1965, p. 746) ‘No battlement, no treasure, nor aught else needs closer guard than women.’ [Euripides] (Harbottle 1897, p. 465) ‘Marriage, if truth be told (of this be sure), an evil is--but one we must endure.’ [Menander] (p. 507)

The Latin thinkers presented the following passages. ''Tis disposition, and not circumstance that makes a woman shameless.' [Seneca] (p. 133) 'Maidens that come dowerless are ever in their husbands' power, but dames with full swollen portions are their plague and rain.' [Plautus] (p. 222)

Montaigne, a French essayist, wrote about wives: 'Or might it not be that opposition and contradiction are in themselves meat and drink to them, and that they are comfortable enough provided they make you uncomfortable' (Montaigne 1965, p. 746).

Schopenhauer wrote. The discord in married life is so frequent that it is the normal state. The normal feeling between men is indifference but between women it is enmity. (Schopenhauer 1962, p. 106) Monogamy with equal rights for both sexes is not fair for men. There is a huge difference of capabilities between them, hence under marriage men's rights are halved and men's duties doubled. (pp. 109, 110)

He further wrote about women. Women are deficient in the power of reasoning and deliberation. They have no sense of justice. They depend upon craft and not on strength, reasoning and deliberation. They have instinctive capacity for cunning and ineradicable tendency to say what is not true. They are inclined to falsity, faithlessness, treachery, ingratitude and so on. (p. 105)

Rousseau wrote: Women have, in general, no love of any art; they have no proper knowledge of any; and they have no genius (p. 107). Rousseau probably meant knowledge in any fields. If we mean the arts we normally associate by art, the reality is so much more striking since a large number of women engage in painting, music and literature.

Most people I spoke with told me that their parents had a marital problem of some sort. It is definitely the fact that good marriages are rare. It is also true that the married people show to the public that their marriage is working well though in fact it is not. This pretension is instinctive and hence universal and possibly originates in the self-preservation of who they are and what they have. The public figures such as politicians and movie stars would try to hide from the public scrutiny that their marriages are on the rocks. These people judge that their unsuccessful marriage would damage their standing in the society.

Marriage promotes stability in the society and to the married people with heavy costs to the people involved. Hence, the government, the firms and the parents want people to be married with kids and settled. The government want the fathers and their sons to be taxpayers during peace and soldiers at the time of war. The firms want the parents and their children as the producers and consumers of commodities. The parents look at their children as continuation of their life. Married people are constrained in many ways, especially financially. They want fixed income and consequently they feel they must keep the jobs, and when there are problems at work they tend to give in to the gain of the employers.

The Third Prophecy is a serious challenge to the people's way of life since the family units have built the civilisations and people are conditioned to think and act on the premise of family life. Majority of people marry thinking that they will be happier, but the fact of the matter after marriage is contrary to that for most of them. This is one way the Third Prophecy makes inroads into people's mind. If people are truly selfish and can analyse the marriage precisely most likely they would not marry.

There are a few views of doing away with marriage institution from history:

Plato in an ideal republic he conjured up proposed to abolish private property and family (Mercer 1996, p. 117).

Epicurus (341 BC-270 BC) preached that people can pursue pleasures as long as they don't go to the extremes. Also he taught people should lead a simple life, avoiding public ambitions and the entanglement of marriage. (p. 130) This Greek philosopher was the founder of Epicureanism and held that the highest good was pleasure.

In around 290 BC, a group of wandering preachers, who were called cynics, appeared in Athens. They showed indifference to riches, honour, freedom, health in their pursuit of virtues. They lived without religion or family. (p. 130)

William Godwin, British political philosopher and novelist, wrote *An Enquiry Concerning Political Justice, and its Influence on General Virtue and Happiness* (1793) and rejected government and political institutions, and marriage. The French Revolution inspired him. He considered marriage as a fraud and a monopoly. (Malthus 1970, pp. 10, 135) It is interesting to note the following developments though he proposed the abolition of marriage in his major work cited above. He married in 1797 to Mary Wollstonecraft, an eminent pioneering feminist. Their daughter, Mary, married Percy Bysshe Shelley, a British romantic poet, in 1816, though both had said they did not believe in marriage, and she wrote the horror novel *Frankenstein* (1818).

Charles Fourier, a French socialist, proposed in his book *Theory of the Four Movements* (1808) that the family as we know be abolished. He argued that instead all people should live in cooperative groups of 100 families. It seems he wanted to introduce free love among the members. He also proposed the abolition of private properties, foreshadowing communist theory by Karl Marx.

Soseki NASTUME proposed his prophecy concerning marriage in his debut novel *I am a Cat* (1905-6). This author is widely acclaimed as the greatest novelist of modern Japan. The early part of his novels and his life showed deep frustration to keep his moral rectitude but later in his life he gained the self-composure coming from the religious thinking. He was deeply unhappy in his married life and it was popularly rumoured that the main reason for this lay in his wife who was reputed to be as bad as Xanthippe, wife of Socrates.

He made a proposition in the above novel that a prophet would appear in the future preaching the futility of marriage. People would thus remain single all their lives, doing away with the institution of marriage. The prophecy's basic concern was the happiness of men who did not have to share the domestic life with women.

Because of the satirical nature of the book, not many people would have taken the message seriously. I have never heard that young people did not want to marry after reading the book. However, I believe the author was genuine in the proposed scheme, though he was married with children and the divorce was not an easy option available to him under the prevailing social customs. I have assessed that the proposal was fatally flawed and unworkable. If he had been given another opportunity of choice between married life and single life, for instance, after a divorce or death of his wife, he would have most likely remarried. He made light of men's overwhelming need for women, especially sexual need, when he made the prophecy, though he referred to young men’s desperate sexual drive in the book. The kind of the social change he proposed must come from the ordinary men not just a small number of men with phenomenally strong will. After cooling off period from the strife he had with his wife, he would have most likely looked for a woman for cohabitation, hoping the things would work out better this time.

Another flaw of his teaching is that he had a family with children, yet he proposed people would not marry in the future. He did not practise the conformance of speech and conduct; hence his persuasive power was very much diminished. We can see the similar instance in the following newspaper report. A drug courier preached people not to work as a drug trafficker, not even to think about it. However vigorous in his preaching, he did it only after the customs officers caught him. Hence his persuasive power was very much reduced.

Another flaw of his proposition lies in the fact that its main theme is happiness of men; males are not generally capable of keeping away from women with willpower. His prophecy is tantamount to the proposal that men would be happier if they keep away from women in the domestic context. This proposal is not attainable for ordinary menfolk. I explain how to cure the nerves in subsequent Section 7 Cure of Nervous Problems. People with nerves cannot cure the problem with willpower because the overwhelming fears. Only way to remove the problem is to grow the part of the brain which did not develop because of the fears administered on them when they were children. In the same manner people cannot keep away from marriage with willpower because of the overwhelming attractions--sexual attraction may be the major--between the sexes before marriage. Only way to remove the urge to marry among the general public is to instil the concept of love towards children. Full growth of the brain cures the nervous disorder completely. In the same way an individual who is convinced of love towards children as I define is determined to be single all its life and if this love spreads to the general public the institution of marriage will all but disappear from the society. The Third Prophecy does not concern itself with the happiness of the believers but focuses its attention solely on the love of the unborn children, which is incomparably stronger than either the self-love or the love between the sexes. Thus the followers of this prophecy can live without women domestically though admittedly not without sex.

None of the above anti-marriage proposals received public acceptance. The parents encouraged their sons and daughters to marry and did not entertain any other thought. Only the new thinking of the Third Prophecy has the strength to live not marrying, having the stronger dictate than any other considerations.

Upon the general foundation of the fateful convention, there are some specific reasons why people marry and have children. People do not normally cite the individual justifications in mind when they decide to tie the knots. They rather think in terms of the aggregate which are superimposed on the concept of the social convention. I am going to enumerate the particular reasons for getting married as follows:

People seek security in marriage. Life can be often harsh and many people think they can be safe within marriage. People can also be lonely at times and they hope that their spouse and children to be born would be good companions.

People want to have children within the sanctity of marriage, thus fulfilling the social aspect of setting up the family. The desire to have children, apart from the need to have sex, may basically come from satisfying their instinct for biological and racial continuity as well as satisfying psychological and social needs. Growth and multiplications are the attributes of all living things, though there are some exceptional circumstances among humans and even among the other living things. Also many people hope, particularly if they are poor, that their children will support them when they get old and can no longer earn a living. Some people who are struggling to make ends meet think that their children can be labour source around the home and business. When people get old, rich or poor, they want their sons and daughters who visit, care about them and become companions. 'Han Fei (Han-fei-tzu) believed that the human beings are on the whole self-interested. He saw the calculation of long-term self-interest and profit even in parents' affection for their children.' (McGreal 1995, p. 45)

The couple fall in love and believe that the cohabitation after marriage ceremony is the only course of action they can take. These sweethearts are afraid that non-marriage may end in an unbearable unhappiness and even separation.

Adolf Hitler wrote that the only purpose of marriage was to have children for the sake of preservation and multiplication of the species and race. In other words, marriage institution was not an end but only the means for the national and racial prosperity. He put forward the above argument based on his totalitarian concept, that is, to place an emphasis on the nation as a whole rather than on the individuals. However, his conviction was at odd with what he did in his personal life; he did not have any child of his own and married his lover just before their deaths.

Men's sexual drive is so strong that they want consenting women in the form of wives around. Whenever men are sexually aroused, instead of looking for suitable and consenting women on every occasion, they grab hold of their wives to satisfy their sexual instinct. This is at least one reason why men want wives around the home.

Referring to the British class system of the 18th century (Mathias 1969, p. 52):

> A spend thrift family or a string of daughters, each of which had to receive part of the estate (or its income) as a dowry, or the absence of any children at all could wreck a family's fortunes and undo the work of several generations of accumulating a landed estate.

'In most societies up to recent times marriage was not primarily a relationship between two individuals, but a social institution, concerned with child rearing, the inheritance and transfer of property and allegiances between different groups in society.' (Whitehouse & Wilkins 1986, p. 164)

Probably people's fear of death plays an important role in deciding to marry and have children. By having children of the same gene, people feel that death does not totally extinguish life but the similar identity in their children carries on further. People are not conscious that the fear of death is one underlying reason for setting up the family, in the same way they are not conscious that they want to preserve their species when they are horny. Instinct dictates these human behaviours.

Section 6 Fear of Death

I am a religious person but do not believe in afterlife. This life metes out all the rewards and punishments of our thoughts and conducts. This has been my approach to the religion from the start till now. As I understand the Bible, the concept of afterlife is not the basic tenet of the Testaments, New as well as Old. Buddhism does not support it either. However, the popular presentations of both religions show Heaven and Hell, not because the presenters believe but because they want to goad the public into their faith. Also fear of death has given rise to the notion of afterlife in the course of human development, especially among the religious, though I believe that the essence of religion has nothing to do with life after death. Many people equate religion with life after death and take the above thinking quite odd. One scholar commented that religion came about because people dreaded death, and the faith in afterlife gave them some consolation they could hang onto. Further many religious people hope that the day of reckoning of the good and the evil must come since these good people tend to lose in the struggle for existence in the society. In the movies and novels, it is the norm that in the end the good are rewarded and the wicked are punished.

Similarly, many people believe that by leaving the children of their blood on earth they can lessen the dreaded thought about death to some extent. Many people feel after having their family that their children will carry on the life, and the torch of life is not entirely extinguished, thus lessening the dread of total void at their expiration. Certainly, the sperm and ovum cells of the parents will keep living in their children, which is biological continuity. The physical and mental characteristics of the progenitors also show up in the progenies, which is racial continuity. I have come to the conclusion that the fear of death is the underlying reason why people have babies, though people may not be conscious of this reasoning when they are making the decision to have children. As a result the same fear is passed to the descendants. In this light and in any other lights, having children is not a recommended practice; the parents are sacrificing their children for their perceived well-being.

Along these lines of thoughts, religion and children played much the same role for some people in alleviating the fear of death. Hence the dread of death must be something very important to human beings, though it is not the only cause for both and does not occupy the human mind in the same way, nor the same people believe in both religion and children.

The fear of death played an important role in shaping the religious thinking and funeral rites of the human race since the ancient times. The ancients might have hoped that if the dead were buried, uncremated, they may come alive in the same way the plant seeds come alive after being buried. This fear will remain in the conscious mind of people even when the Third Prophecy dominates the thinking of the people: Rather people may be more worried about death because the other problems of the society are reduced or eliminated. Animals, whether they are conscious of death or not, try to preserve their life in the best way they can. The characteristics of all the living things are the preservation of their life and the desire to multiply the same kind, and the fear of death and the sexual desire among the other myriads of human thoughts help achieve these goals.

Classical Judaism does not have any concept of afterlife as the books of Ecclesiastes and Job show. However, an afterlife as a concept was introduced into Judaism during the Hellenistic period (323-30 BC), as the books of Isaiah and Daniel make references. Still the idea does not form the fundamental tenet of Judaism and Christianity. The following verses clearly show that the essence of Christianity is not about afterlife.

Jesus Christ said:

> The kingdom of God is not coming with things that can be observed; nor will they say, 'Look, here it is! or There it is!' For, in fact, the kingdom of God is within you (Luke 17:21).

We find the similar verses in the Old Testament as the above saying:

> Now what I am commanding you today is not too difficult for you or beyond your reach (Deuteronomy 30:1).
> No, the word is very near you: it is in your mouth and in your heart so you may obey it (Deuteronomy 30:14).

We find the following passages in the New Testament:

> 'I am the God of Abraham, the God of Isaac, and the God of Jacob.' He is God not of the dead, but of the living. (Matthew 22:32)

However, Paul wrote in spite of the above passages that people are resurrected spiritually after death (1 Corinthians 15:35-58).

The Qur'an (Koran) clearly states the existence of afterlife as reward and punishment of this life. In fact the concept of reward and punishment in the afterlife is the repeated and central message of Islam. For example, the Qur'an says:

> Every soul shall have a state of death: and only on the day of judgement shall you be paid your full recompense. Only he who is saved far from the Fire and admitted to the Garden will have attained the object of life: for the life of this world is but goods and chattels of deception. (Qur'an 3.185)

Nirvana of Buddhism may be equated to the Kingdom of God or Heaven of Christianity. Similarly Buddhist purgatory may be equated with Christian Sheol (or Hell) or the ancient Greek Hades. As I understand, Heaven and Hell are symbolic expressions of happiness and unhappiness of this world, which depends on the morality of the individuals. I can also see that the concept was used to goad ancient people who were mostly illiterate and superstitious to the path of goodness.

The Buddha taught that the reason why people suffer is that they try to satisfy five senses; they want popularity or worldliness; they want eternal life and fear death. He asserted all these desires are evil. Buddhism as the Buddha taught clearly does not support the concept of afterlife.

I used to be afraid of death since I was a small child, so small as I slept with my mother. I kept thinking what would happen to me after I died. The thought that I no longer existed after expiration terrified me. I could not bear the notion that there was nothing to recognise me as such. It was hard to imagine what it was like to have a void instead of thinking self. Shakespeare compared death to sleep with some reservation in the soliloquy by Hamlet as I quoted earlier. Many centuries earlier Socrates compared death to sleep without any dreams (Guthrie 1969, p. 479), not believing in afterlife. I could grasp the terror only for a brief moment and then I clang to my mother's arm in an effort to have some relief. I was fully aware that my mum could not have helped me in any way and did not even tell the problem to her. To think back now, my relationship with my parents should have been such that I felt free to ask their opinions. If our family had been on good speaking terms at that time, the dreadful family breakdown at the later years would not have happened. When I mentioned the terror of death to a couple of my primary school mates, they both perceived my emotional state correctly but dismissed my concern, saying that they were not afraid since they would not feel anything in being dead.

The feeling of sheer dread of death experienced for a brief moment lasted for many years--until well into adolescence. I simply could not accept the fate of humans that the thinking self ceased to exist at death; a total obliteration of permanence. We wake up after a sleep but with death we do not wake up forever: I simply could not work out the mechanism. Many religions teach that people go to Heaven or Hell after expiration depending on their ethical conducts in this world. Though I was unreligious at the time, I knew that many religions promised certain things including the afterlife. However, the promise was utterly useless for me. The terror struck me at any time; when walking along the street, talking to somebody or reading a book. However, the sense of fear diminished when I reached to a certain age. I did not direct my mind to this state but I simply outgrew it after many years. The dread does not trouble me anymore. I can think about death and face it squarely without a flinch. Only time I am afraid is when I am half-asleep, the notion of a void after death as I remember suddenly grips me and I feel frightened in the same intensity as before: I cannot get into this state intentionally. Bertrand Russell taught that we should not overcome fear of any kind by willpower but we should naturally lead ourselves to the loss of interest in what we were afraid of. This was precisely what happened to me concerning the fear of death.

People fear death universally. We cannot dismiss the fear of death simply as phobia since it explains some of the human behaviours. However, the terrifying emotion I went through lying beside my mother was unusual in its strength at such a tender age. We do not have any fright about the fact we had not existed before we were born. We are only worried about our thinking self after death. It is absolutely true that once we are dead there is no fear at all because there is no conscious self to start with. Probably the anticipation of death is more frightful than the death itself.

I vaguely remember an essay I read when I was a secondary school student. It said there were no skills which cannot be made easier by practice: we can overcome even the fear of death if we try with vigilance. Probably I practised the skill unintentionally and grew out of the dread. We can practise virtually everything to attain proficiency. As far as the process of dying is concerned, we cannot practise because we go through only once in our life (Montaigne 1965, p. 267), though many people speak about near-death experience.

Montaigne, an essayist, wrote that death comes easier in the battlefield than at home. He drew that conclusion after having witnessed many people die both in battles and during peace time.

> Now I have often pondered how it happens that in wars the face of death, whether we see it in ourselves or in others, seems to us incomparably less terrifying than in our houses ... (p. 67).

I certainly knew from my own experience that under the extreme tension of fist fights the body blows received did not have much impact on me during the struggle. After the fight I assessed what damage was done on my physique and started feeling pains. In the similar reasoning, we are not so much frightened of dying when subjected to everyday struggle for existence. Perhaps we should be thankful for the various problems of life, without which we would be ever fearful of death.

The same author made an interesting comment which contradicts his statement in another part:

> If we don't know how to live a good life, it is wrong to dwell how to die. Death is an end, finish and extremity and not the goal or object of life. (p. 805)

Japanese Monk

I remember reading a story of a Japanese Buddhist who organised himself to be kept alive in an underground ventilated hole until he would starve to death. The describing magazine said that the idea of the above setup was to make a mummy of his body. The ancient Egyptians made mummies of their bodies in the hope of resurrection in the centuries to come. Obviously this Japanese monk did not believe in the resurrection. He had eaten, prior to the burial, certain kinds of food to help mummification process.

He kept hitting *mokugyo* as long as he was alive in the underground chamber, thus telling people on the ground that he was still alive. They knew he was dead when they no longer heard the hitting sound. The magazine carried a photograph of his mummified body. There was no sign that he died struggling. He was sitting erect, cross-legged, his head being slightly bent forward. The magazine stated only the above fact but did not mention why he did it in the first place. What was the true intent of the monk in doing thus? Was he silly enough to make a mummy of himself in order to preserve his body for the future exhibition? It occurred to me one day that he might have wanted to show people that he had overcome the fear of death. Thus he might have wished to spread to the world the greatness of Buddhism, through which he had attained the desired state of mind.

Whatever might have been his motive in the venture, I have no doubt that he did not have any fear of dying at all.

Nature of Fear

Fear of death was certainly different in nature from another terror which my father used to deliver on me from time to time. It is hard to break up and analyse the characteristics of the two fears, one from the speculation of life and death and the other from the capriciousness of my father. I feel these dreaded feelings were received and stored in the same part of my brain. Both were frightening to the extreme and shattered my brain, possibly, irreparably, in the absence of proper guidance. Looking back these experiences today, I have no doubt the extreme fright arrested the proper development of my personality. Also I have come to believe that fear became the driving force of my life. Fear of failure compelled me to study and succeed. When there was no fear, there was no motivation hence no effort. This mental attitude was unfortunate for anyone to have, displaying the negative aspect of life. However, on the positive note, both fears, I believe, goaded me towards justice in my personal life as well as in the world. I wanted to see justice done at all times at any levels, personal and social. I almost always chose what was morally right and avoided what was evil.

When I grew up I took revenge on my dad for the fears he instilled in me--most of the time without justification. He would have never treated me as he did, had he known that what dreaded consequence his brutish behaviour brought on my personality and life as well as how mercilessly I would retaliate on him later in our lives. There was no bond established between us since my childhood hence the revenge came naturally to me and was possibly the only proper course of action I could take. I firmly believe that what I did on him later in our lives was less than what he had done on me in my childhood.

I still remember an episode concerning the fear administered by my father, though the fear from my father was a constant consciousness in my childhood. When a family doctor was attending my physical sickness of some sort at my place, it happened from the circumstances that I mentioned to him I kept away from home for some time to avoid to be scolded by my father for a minor offence. This doctor was very much surprised what he heard and tried to get the full story, though my mother sitting beside us tried to prevent. After knowing what was happening at my place, the doctor asked her to meet him in another room. My mother later told what she heard from him to the family including my father and me. According to the doctor, it was wrong to frighten a small child since the development of its mentality would be arrested and would show up as a nervous problem in its later life. Being encouraged by this development, on the next incident I defied my father, insisting that my mother was at fault. All he did was to give me a fright which I would never forget nor forgive my parents for the rest of my life. Though the incident itself became a minor memory in my childhood it came back haunting me as I grew older.

Mencius was only three when his father died. His mother moved their residence several times until settling near a school so that Mencius as a boy had a right model to imitate. She also cut the cloth in her loom in his presence. She taught him the lesson that he had to have perseverance and devotion in his studies in the same way she had to with the loom. Traditionally Mencius' mother was held as the model mother in China.

I have come to believe that my mother was greater than Mencius' and taught me greater lessons to me. She by her stupidity taught me what women are like and to keep away from women domestically, if I want to be happy. Every time I had a conflict with my mother, my father always sided with her for unknown reasons to me and frightened me. He used to tell me that unless we look at women as inferior we always get angry with them. He had been with her a long time before I was born and still with her after I deserted them. Probably he could not work out the reason why he had to put up with her for so many years as many men have wondered why through the millenniums but could not work out. In fact the answer lies in the Third Prophecy with its uncontaminated love for their children: only after people learn to love their own children as I define it becomes the only logical and unfailing consequence that they keep away from women domestically.

I confirmed later in my life what my mother taught me. However, when some women on occasions behaved nicely to me I cannot work out what to make of them. It must be the rule that men do not know what to make of them when some women behave nicely, and some of them decide to get married irrespective of what hold in the married life.

Fears of death come from life itself for the thinking minds like humans. Animals do not speculate the dread philosophically: they do not think about death beforehand when there is no danger to their life but they sense the fear moments before death. They have offspring in the same way as humans do but they cannot explain why they do: we normally attribute their offspring bearing processes to instinct. The fact that people are afraid of death and possible way of eliminating the fear of death are the topic of this section.

Death Makes Everyone Equal.

Everyone is equal in the face of death. If we think that all the sufferings of life, whatever they may be, will end when we die, they become a bit more bearable. Since we don't have consciousness after expiration, it is not really important who we are or what we are. What we achieve in life or even whether we are morally good or bad are nothing at all if we reflect we have to die sooner or later.

Julius Caesar (100-44 BC) was once asked what death was most desirable and he replied 'the least meditated and the quickest' (Montaigne 1965, p. 460). Thus he effectively admitted he was afraid of death and pains associated with dying. He brought enormous sufferings and deaths to a large number of people by his campaigns for the sake of Rome and his ambitions, and did not think anything to bring them to the other people. Possibly he never thought that he could conquer the fear of death by constant effort in the similar reasoning that Caesar and his Roman army could conquer the world as he might have imagined.

The First Emperor (Shih huang-ti) (c. 259-c. 210 BC) completed the Great Wall of China which was built to be the bulwark against nomadic incursions. Among so many of his achievements which marvel us even the modern people, some scholars insist that his script reform be his greatest achievement, by which means the Chinese people have communicated on paper through the millenniums until the present day. Since his reform, successive generations in China have used a single form of written characters overriding various dialects. (Oliphant 1992, p. 170; Toynbee 1962, p. 603)

In spite of or I might say because of his illustrious career, Shih huang-ti had one fatal weakness: he was very much afraid of death. He had more than 20 children and according to legend, he was a formidable lover endowed with enormous sexual prowess and had many beautiful women brought to his court from all over China. (Guisso & Pagani 1989, p. 20) In the course of unification he sacrificed a huge number of people, friends and foes, and obviously he did not regard the other people's lives in the same light as his own. The search for immortality was a recurrent and constant theme in his life. (p. 140) He kept full-time alchemists at court working continually to synthesise the sacred herbs (p. 172). In a desperate wish to prolong his life, he dispatched envoys with the mission to acquire elixir of immortality. One story goes like this:

> ..., and along the way met a group of magicians who begged for permission to mount an expedition to the fairy islands of Penglai to find the elixir of immortality. Delighted with the idea, Shihuang [Shih huang-ti] sent the magicians out with a conscripted force of 'thousands of youths and maidens' to find the mysterious potion. To the best of our knowledge, they never returned. (p. 132)
>
> Note: Penglai is a port city in Shandong (Shantung) Province and the city is traditionally a fabled spot where the immortals are said to have made appearance. The above fairy islands refer to the islands just north of Penglai city.

This elixir of life is conceptually the same as the tree of life in the Garden of Eden (Genesis 2:9) and both are supposed to confer eternal life. Also the Bible describes a tree of life as a figure of speech of wellbeing: She [wisdom] is a tree of life to those who embrace her; those who lay hold of her will be blessed (Proverbs 3:18). The modern people may sympathise with Shih huang-ti's longing for eternal life and at the same time scoff at his rather crude way of trying to achieve it, though a small number of people today are attracted to Fountain of Youth whose waters, they are led to believe, could cure ills and renew youth. However, the emperor was quite serious about the mission, though nobody presented him with the desired substance.

His approach to try to solve the problem of the fear of death is quite materialistic: he looked for the material (elixir of immortality; drugs or herbs). His way of thinking was by various evidence directed to materials. He could have been successful if he had directed his mind inwards to train himself not to be fearful of death. The fear of death was a challenge to him and his response was to prolong his life with substance. He did not try to eliminate the fear itself as many thinkers tried and some succeeded. Though he would not have lived for eternity as he wished erroneously still he could have removed the fear of death.

Ssu-ma Ch'ien vividly describes in his memorable book *Shih-chi* how Shih huang-ti narrowly escaped the assassination plot Ching Ko carefully engineered. As a matter of fact, he had several assassination attempts on his life. He took these incidents to his heart, especially the attempt by Ching Ko which nearly succeeded. (Chien 1979, pp. 392-402) They made him even more afraid of death; thence he tended to avoid contact with people (Fryer 1975, pp. 47-8). His limited audience with his subjects naturally brought about a shift of his governing style and policy. The emperor died in 210 BC on a tour in search for the elixir of immortality. (Guisso & Pagani 1989, p. 37) It is largely through the above book, sometimes referred to as *The Records of the Grand Historian of China*, that we learn anything of the life of Shih huang-ti.

The foregoing episodes show that these conquering heroes were no different from the ordinary folks of the contemporary society and even today as far as the fear of death was concerned; they were afraid to die in the same way any other people were. They were practical people and did not think, as philosophers might have thought, that a proper guidance could eliminate the fear of death. There is another common thread in these heroes which strikes us quite illogical: they did not care about the other people's lives and slaughtered a large number of people for the empire and their personal glory.

Many people say that they believe in life after death. This belief may be religious or non-religious. Apart from the concept of afterlife, a surprisingly large number of people tell that they believe in reincarnations: they think they lived as different persons before the present life and that they will be reborn as other persons. Most of these people, strangely enough, fear death, which may suggest that their testimony may not be genuine or they may be afraid of the unknown, as the toddlers are of the dark. In any case, the belief in afterlife or reincarnation removes fear from death to some extent.

When we are exposed to a certain type of disease, we normally develop natural resistance to the disease if we are fortunate enough to recover; we are less likely to suffer from the same disease in the future. In the same logic, if we are exposed to fear of death, we naturally develop the way of thinking which makes the fear less frightening. It took approximately 15 years before the major anxiety concerning death disappeared from my conscious mind. I don't think I can pass that knowledge to other people since I cannot explain the eliminating process in any language. I am sure many people, particularly those exposed to religion and philosophy, tried to eliminate the dread of death systematically, though each individual had to devise its own means to achieve the end. In the same way the enlightenments the Buddha and Jesus Christ reached cannot be imparted to the other people, and they can give out only the material we can work on.

Section 7 Cure of Nervous Problems

Mental disorders cover a huge variety of illnesses with recognisable psychological or behavioural manifestations and are sometimes referred to as mental ill-health or psychiatric illnesses. Mental disorders are broadly classed, unsatisfactorily, into neuroses and psychoses. Psychotic patients who are not capable of functioning the everyday life and not aware they have serious problems have more severe symptoms than neurotic patients who can function the everyday chores and are aware that they have a problem. The mental disorders may be due to psychological, social, biochemical, or genetic dysfunction or disturbance. No single theory of causation explains all mental disorders.

Personality disorders, though they come under mental disorders, do not belong to neuroses or psychoses.

Some mental disorders such as Alzheimer's disease are clearly caused by organic disease of the brain. Some mental disorders are caused by the arrest of the mental growth in childhood. This section deals only with the latter disorders and prominently manifested as inhibited speech, depression, delinquency, obsessive and schizoid character, hysterical disorders and some forms of phobia. We must stress that the other causes might have brought the latter disorders. It is widely agreed that the nervous problem is typical of the disorder due to arrested growth of the patients. Nervous disorder is a euphemism that covers a whole range of psychoneuroses and psychoses. The nervous disorders manifest in the various ways in a large number of people who are anxious to live without the problem but don't know how.

Sigmund Freud (1856-1939), an Austrian psychiatrist, is recognised as the founder of psychoanalysis. That every patient resists treatment by psychoanalysis, that is, treatment which operates through the acquisition of self-knowledge, was perhaps Freud's most important discovery. (Guntrip 1964, p. 117) Thus in psychotherapy the therapist-patient relationship is the key to the nature and success of the treatment (p. 129). Therein lies the difficulty of the patient being able to accept treatment. It is hard to admit that one's problems are due to the fact that some of one's personality still carries the legacy of childhood so literally that one actually feels and reacts as a child in that part of the self. (p. 131)

Freud concluded that many of his patients behaved according to their subconscious minds, that is, drives and experiences of which they are not consciously aware. The childhood memories constitute much of the subconscious of the adults; however, if their memories are especially painful, the patients build defence mechanism to keep out of conscious awareness. The strong defence mechanism ties up huge energy which impedes the proper development of the patients' minds, causing neurosis, a form of mental illness. Freud considered psychiatric symptoms the result of misdirection or inadequate discharge of libido. Freud, in the process of treating the neurotic patients, realised that the free association, in which the patient relaxes and relates to the therapist whatever comes to mind, gives an important clues to the subconscious mind of the patient. (Westheimer 1994, p. 117) He also contended that the patients' dreams give out the clues to subconscious feelings. It is interesting to note that *Interpretation of Dreams* (1900), perhaps his greatest work, came out of the above theorisation and not an accidental research.

Every dream has a meaning as a psychical structure, which can be interpreted with a psychological technique. That meaning is related to the mental activities of the waking life--immediate or long past. (Freud 1982, p. 1) Dreams can represent reality in symbols (p. 7). Nothing which we have once mentally possessed can be entirely lost. The human memory thus acquired plays major role in waking life as well as in dreams. Memories stored while infants as well as the events in the previous day play parts in the material of dreams. Often memories which are not on our conscious minds play major roles in dreaming. (p. 20) Our scientific consideration of dreams starts off from the assumption that they are products of our own mental activity. The scene of action in dream is different from that of waking ideational life. (p. 48) The mental activity between falling asleep and waking up is illusory, though during sleep we think that dream-images are real. Detachment from the external world seems to be the major attribute of the dreams. (pp. 51-2) In sleep the mind isolates itself from the external world and withdraws from its own periphery. Nevertheless the connection is not broken off entirely. (p. 53) Impulses and passions lead the dreams, and conscience is mostly pushed away. In the real life the above positions are mostly reversed. In both dreams and realities there are no rigid laws governing the impulses, passions and conscience. (p. 73) In dreams, we have only partial control of psychical activity and no control on somatic activity (p. 76). Freud expounded on symbolic dream interpretation as the decoding method (p. 97).

We must extract the latent dream thoughts from the manifest content of dreams (p. 277). We must remember that the dream thoughts are often the results of the subconscious thought process (p. 281). The principal components of the dream and those of the dream thoughts are often not the same. This is the work of displacement, one of the dream works. (p. 305) Dream-condensation and dream-displacement are the two governing principles to untangle the dreams (p. 308). The dream work may bring in the dream symbols which must be correctly interpreted (p. 353). The dream contents have various events fused into one action: dream-condensation (p. 179). If I am afraid of robbers in a dream, the robbers are imagery but the fear can be real. The emotions in the dreams do not necessarily correspond to the emotions of the dreamer. The fear in the dream may or may not create the fear in the dreamer. (p. 460)

Freud postulated the following psychological stages of development for the children: the oral stage, the anal stage and the phallic stage. He postulated that the neurotic patients did not go through each stage successfully with the normal resolution of the urges. I give the detailed descriptions of these stages under the heading of 'Psychological Stages of Development by Freud' in Section 1 Sexual Desire, Chapter 1, Book Five *The Sexual Laws*.

Today we know the family to be the key member of our institutions, and it is widely accepted that much of our society's sickness, in particular crime and neurosis, is directly traceable to something that went wrong within the family. The reluctance to admit on the part of the parents that they had the problem within the family has the parallel on the part of the patient to admit its problem. The ultimate issue facing psychotherapy today is the issue of whether, if a basically strong ego was not formed in childhood, its lack can be remedied by any therapeutic procedure in later life. (Guntrip 1964, pp. 143, 191)

Confucius' primary concern was about the family--filial piety and education of children. Though Confucianism at present is not a dominant teaching anywhere in the world, its focus was correct as far as removing the woes of both the society and neurotic people were concerned. Also Montaigne wrote the following sentence drawing the conclusion from his own experience:

> I find that our greatest vices take shape from our tenderest childhood, and that our most important training is in the hands of nurses (Montaigne 1965, p. 78).

Freud contended that an adult's social relationships are patterned after the early family relationships. Most social scientists today accept this view.

The social issues and neurotic problems have deep roots in the way of life, and to cure the problems people have to change their thinking process and their way of life.

Healing the Sick Mind (1964) by H Guntrip, a British doctor, describes the treatments which the extremely nervous patients can cure of the problem. According to this book, the root cause of the nerves is an arrested growth as toddlers, resulting from fear administered most likely by their fathers. Fear is the worst of all emotions to arouse in a child (Guntrip 1964, p. 72):

> Arousal of strong fear in a child blocks the normal and natural process of self-development. This child tends to withdraw into himself and does not respond to his surroundings.

As a consequence, the children's minds do not grow normally when measured in mental age, though certainly they are no different from other kids physically and intellectually. Unless these affected children are treated properly, their brains do not mature as they should. Instead these patients rely on fantasies to avoid the harsh realities of the society, and their thoughts wander aimlessly. The day dreams and night dreams are the thoughts wandering without purpose or direction. They shut themselves within their dream world and they remain helpless small children even as the years go on. Psychologically, this state is termed regression: the grown-ups adopt this behaviour more appropriate to a child, as a defence mechanism to avoid anxiety.

The mental ill-health of this kind is manifested in psychoneurosis or commonly called nerves and its extreme form is called psychosis (p. 17). Psychoneuroses manifest as obsessions, hysteric conditions, anxiety states, and the social phobias of various kinds: blushing, stammering and awkward manner in the public. Psychoses, withdrawn deeper, manifest as schizophrenics, maniac-depressive states and paranoid conditions. (p. 93) Instead of looking at the parts of personality, such as symptoms and habits, we have to shift the emphasis of treatment to the total self or whole personality. This approach is termed whole personality therapy. (p. 189) The cure is to stop the habit of dreaming and let their minds develop naturally. This curing approach may take time to have effect, as the author emphasises, but is the only and certain way to treat the suffering patients at whatever age they may be.

The root cause of all personality disturbances, Guntrip argues, is the degree of mental withdrawnness, due to primary fears, which has become a relatively permanent feature of the patient’s personality (p. 209). The withdrawn people tend to live more and more in the inner world of the mind, and as their detachment from outer realities grows greater, their inner world becomes more and more a bizarre anxiety-ridden fantasy world (p. 210). Troublesome sexual and aggressive impulses at least enable the mental patient to feel strong (p. 185). As the toddlers are prone to tantrums, the neurotic patients burst into fits of angers. Though the children normally do not know how to release themselves sexually, the grown patients indulge in the fantasies, sexual and non-sexual, and sex. Also the patients show a strong sense of love and hate, as the children do.

There is another approach to remove the nervous problems. *Dianetics: the Modern Science of Mental Health* (1985) by LR Hubbard mentions the curing process by which means to remove the charged engrams of the patients. Dianetics is a form of psychotherapy originated by Hubbard and a forerunner of Scientology which he founded in 1954. When the minds are usefully employed by the owners, the thought is in its right connection of the analytical mode and the owners naturally get the benefits in due course. Deranged persons are those who have had the wrong thinking process lasting for many years with the various engrams intact though some engrams were planted prenatally. These are the persons who did not think in a correct way and let their minds drift in aimless manners of the reactive mode. Only way to cure the deranged persons, Hubbard lectures, will be to have the right circuit for some years. Hubbard goes beyond curing the deranged persons and teaches that the normal persons can get benefits by correct electrical connection in their brains and these people will become mature and competent over the years.

I believe that both of the aforementioned techniques correctly describe the cure of nervous disorders in two seemingly different approaches, which suggests that they were developed independently. They both stress that the nervous problems could disappear without a trace as long as the patients observe their prescriptions correctly for some time to take effect.

The problem of the long suffering patients of the nervous nature is that they do not see the fundamental cause as outlined above but rather they try to overcome their nerves by focusing their attention on the manifestations of the problems. They somehow convince themselves that they can suppress the nervous attacks with willpower or even with religious faith. They don't understand that the root cause lies somewhere else. Willpower and religious faith will help them if these are used to remove the root problem. It is recognised that the suppression of the symptoms can be useful for short term rehabilitation only but definitely not a cure. (Guntrip 1964, p. 180)

Why Was This Section Presented?

Since I am not a medical doctor, I should not give out any medical advice. Also this series of the books are addressed to the average readers, dealing only with the matters of ordinary occurrences. However, I have come to believe that a large proportion of the world population have the problem of nerves and a vast majority of people have some kind of mental ill-health though not pronounced. I am not here to give a medical advice but am pointing out the problems and the cures as the few authorities in this field described. This section is an insight for the average readers who have some dealings with a nervous problem.

The main reason why this curing technique is introduced in this book is that the major problems of the human race cannot be tackled directly as for the nervous problems, the causes of these problems lying deeper and in fact somewhere else. Singing Beethoven's song 'We are all brothers', however enthusiastically, does not promote the harmonious relationship among humans. Tackling the problems head-on gives only the temporary relief. As I explain in this section, the correction of the whole personality is the cure of the nerves and nothing else will help the patients in the long run. The same thing can be said about the corrections of the various problems of the human race. I expound in Section 3, Chapter 3 that we cannot remove the evils of wars and women with willpower but only the practice of the Third Prophecy will cure the problems. Also I show in the same chapter that only the Third Prophecy has the capacity to solve the various problems which idealism and materialism tackled head-on but gave only partial solution. I must stress again that we cannot solve the problems of nerves and social ills permanently by tackling the problems with willpower but we must look for the solution somewhere else. We may see the phenomena as the problems but must mend the way we think to solve the problems, which is in fact in accord with the religious teachings.

Chapter 2 Idealism and Materialism before Spread of the Third Prophecy

Section 1 General Survey

I explore idealism and materialism fully in conjunction with the historical developments in Book One.

The fact that the social reforms of the various intents, in the main, failed through the centuries made many historical figures believe that the society as we know would never change no matter what would happen in the future. Montaigne in his *Essays* wrote that all social reforms failed and nobody changed the social system for the better. Balzac was sarcastically insistent that people had never changed through many happenings in history. Confucius repeatedly stated that his contemporary humans were a lot worse than the people of the earlier era. These are some of the opinions about the status of the society and nobody can prove or disprove the validities of their assertions.

This is the only section where I refer to Balzac (1799-1850), a French novelist, in this series of books. A few words here about him may be in order. He was conscious of his own genius and his writings show sarcasm, wit and psychological observation. He is regarded as the creator of realism or naturalism in novels and acknowledged as the man who established the technique of the orthodox modern novel.

Probably we should delve into what aspects of the human activities they were referring to before we can comment on their opinions. Montaigne was talking about the society as he lived through as well as the ancient to classical societies, particularly Roman and Greek, he knew well through reading a vast amount of literature; Balzac to the characteristics of the human beings; Confucius to the human conducts which were his primary concern. These historical persons before the modern era were not aware that the human races would make a tremendous advance in the spheres of science and technology in the future and did not even dream that technology would one day govern their societies, not the social system, nor human nature, nor ethics as these characters imagined or hoped. As the result of the tremendous technical advancement in the recent years, the outcome of war more or less depends on the technical levels of the weapons the combatants use, rather than on ethics, religious or economic ideologies, or even the economic strength, as were the case in the past. It is true that the sense of righteousness and will to fight, their abundance and quality or their paucity, have decided the outcomes of many wars through the human history--even today--superimposed on the above qualities. No individual today doubt that the society has improved and will improve vastly as far as scientific and medical knowledge together with technologies is concerned. These people above quoted formed their opinions under the societies they lived and if they look at the modern technical marvels, they may alter their suppositions.

There have been numerous reforms throughout human history as attempts to impose justice in the community. The natures of reforms seem to me as numerous as the countless number of improvements undertaken, each exhibiting its own characteristics. However, we characterise these attempts in such descriptions as religious, economic, legal, social, and political, the characterisations depicting only the chief focus of concern. Reforms in this section, though for argument sake only, refer to attempts for improvement on a social scale: voluntary or forced; radical or gradual; intended or unintended. Hence they include not only those used in an ordinary sense but revolutions, wars of independence and unintended social changes.

Historians tell us whether a particular reform was a success or a failure. On a continuum from success to failure, as far as I understand history, successful reforms were rare in comparison with unsuccessful ones and also the many successful reforms remained so for a short while to be overpowered by new happenings. There have been a lot of well-meaning attempts to correct the wrongs of a nation but they have been mostly used or hampered by the corrupt people or by the people who had the vested interest in the existing order. Reforms which produced permanent good results may be said to be a few drops in the ocean of corruptions.

The social reforms generally did little to improve the social conditions; however, the failures of the various attempts in the past do not mean they will fail in the future. The social reforms succeeded only when they suited the people concerned, not because their aims were just or right. I do believe that the new society where the Third Prophecy prevails has many right conditions for a better human society. Readers should judge for themselves the validities of my assertion, after reading this book, that the new society as I propose is a lot better off, idealistically and materialistically, than the society of today mostly governed by the acquisition of necessities of life, sex, religion, idealism, materialism, racism, nationalism, sexism and arts.

I present idealism and materialism in Book One as the two major ideologies of the human kind. The concept of the Third Prophecy has nothing to do with either of them, but it, as I see, will eventually lead to the fulfilment of what religion and Marxism proposed but failed to deliver. In the new society where the bulk of the population practise the ideal of the Third Prophecy, people's way of life will be characterised by the abundance of idealistic conducts as well as the plethora of goods and services, without being worried about the depletion of natural resources and the environmental damages.

I will assure readers that people, without exception, cannot escape the fate of human beings that even in the new society they will all suffer and die as in any societies in the past and present.

What is the society like under idealism and materialism in terms of everyday life? What happens in our life is so varied that I may not be able to answer the question meaningfully. I will try to indicate what the society, past and present, has been like before the introduction of the Third Prophecy since it gives us the starting point for comparison and contrast. The new society will come under sharper focus in the next chapter.

Most of the daily dealings in our life do not correspond to the teachings of the Bible. Daily struggle for existence is so harsh that many people cannot incorporate the messages of the two Testaments, particularly the concept ‘Love thy neighbour’, when conducting day to day business. People who followed the moral codes to the letter as the Ten Commandments represent were ever a tiny minority throughout human history. It is often the case that the incompetent and untalented people have dominated the families, firms and nations, pushing away the competent and talented people.

Even in the twelfth century Europe when the papal authority reached zenith, I believe that the Christians in the truest sense were hard to find, though a large number of people professed to belong to the Christian denominations. I would say that people around that time conducted the business in much the same way as the people do in the modern society. People lied, cheated, bribed and played dirty tricks to get ahead of other people. They also tried to escape due blames and punishments when what they had done turned out to be mistakes. They did not behave correctly even when there was no need to do so. A small number of people who did not follow the general practice (lying, cheating, bribery and trickery) were left behind and often did not get what they wanted though they were entitled to. The Christian way of life did not and does not explain what the society has been like in everyday dealings.

If we turn our attention to the organisations (private and governmental) in the present society, the situations are not much different. It is true that to get a good job people must be properly qualified and experienced but it is also true that people must tell convincing lies at the interview to become ahead of the other applicants. I have learned in my bitter experience that transfers and promotions were more to do with Machiavellianism than the real fitness of the individuals. When there is a mistake of whatever kind in an organisation, in many cases people do not know who made the mistake because of lots of lies circulating.

The following are the wisdom of the world going against idealism which a small number of people have cherished; nonetheless the worldly wisdom is in wide circulation and applicable both in the organisations and outside:

- You don't get anything, e.g., a position, unless you do something (lie, cheat, bribe or trick) about it.
- If people catch your weakness once, you are finished within the organisation. Therefore if you make a serious mistake, you must place the blame on somebody else. You cannot hide habitual hesitancy in writing and speech hence you have to overcome these habits at any cost.
- At the time of conflicts, if people proceed with honesty, they lose. All the people under conflict tell lies, hence you must tell lies to be par with the opponents.
- The bosses will tell lies and all sorts of bullshits because many of them are not capable to lead--with not enough experience or not enough theoretical background. Unless you complain, your supervisors will do anything on you, hence you must complain.
- You have to make sure that any happenings in the firm or in the general community do not get to you. The idealists often emphasise this rule when you are on the right. However, it is applicable, according to the wisdom of the world, even when you are on the wrong.
- The minority, racially and sexually, in the community, the production personnel in the manufacturing environment and the foot soldiers in the army do the tricks when they have a chance to do, though they are often pushed aside from the decision-making process. Therefore you have to do the tricks when you have a chance to do.
- Everyone tries to get as much as possible, otherwise they lose something they are entitled to.

  The problem is that people try to get what they are not entitled to. All the people go as far as they can go: they try to get everything they can get hold of. For example, in the corporative environment, the employees get to know what is the tolerance limit of the firm or how far they can go before being dismissed. They always go to that limit when they are lazy or not following the orders from above, no more and no less.
- The managers want an employee who is good at talking whether its contents can be lies rather than a worker who is good at doing jobs. Hence it is beneficial to improve the conversational skills rather than the job skills.
- Instead of working hard, it is often easier to curry favour your superiors to get promotion.
- When you want to take upper hand over somebody, it is often the best you base the strategy on lies. It does not matter if that person lives in accord with justice or injustice.

The religious, the Buddhists and the Christians alike, tend to lose in the struggle for existence when pitted against the foregoing rules.

The Buddhist scripture gives out the following stanza:

> Surely, the path that leads to worldly gain is one, and the path that leads to Nibbana [nirvana] is another; understanding this, the bhikkhu [bhiksu], the disciple of the Buddha, should not rejoice in worldly favours, but cultivate detachment. Detachment is threefold: bodily separation from the people; mental separation from passions; complete separation from all conditioned things. (Narada 1993, p. 72)

Confucius repeatedly denounced his contemporary society and urged people to return to the ethical level of the golden age of the Chou dynasty which he idolised. The political and social instability characterised his contemporary society which was entering into the warring period; however, he did not know that the quest for truths such as the moral codes came to ardent concerns by the serious thinkers such as Confucius himself, Mencius and Lao-tzu, only when the general public went through deep sufferings. In other words, the prominent philosophers of the time were products of political and social turmoils, without which these people could not have developed their unique way of solving the problem of deep unhappiness. In the first place, without deep sufferings the problems did not exist and people did not have to look for the way to escape. He also did not realise that the human relationships during the height of the Chou dynasty, as we can infer from the human nature, were essentially no different from those of his era. He did not base his opinions on the objective observations but rather he formed them through the sacred books he read and venerated, and the idealised picture of the golden era of Chou firmly got hold of him. These observations can be supported by the fact that he admitted openly that his ideas of ethics were not of his making but taken from the sacred books of the Chou era.

I am sure that human dealings have been, in part, decided, in the East as well as in the West, through the ages on such principles as 'Dogs eat dogs', 'Might is right' or 'Machiavellianism'. These principles were superimposed on the qualities often talked about in the open culture, that is, educational qualifications, experiences and capabilities of the people. The above statement is the only logical conclusion I can draw from my life experience as well as the speculations. Certainly we don't know how the events would turn up in each case but there are no alternatives to the above judgement since everyone wants as much as they can get under the set condition, being prepared to sacrifice the welfares of other people.

The communist view does not explain life or the world either. The communist theories may sound fantastic at first hearing but they do not stand the scrutiny of even superficial nature, as I present in Book Three *Communism*. I found that many propositions of Karl Marx were correct only partially and some outright wrong conceptually. As I made a probe into his personal life, I found that he did not live in accordance with his politico-economic theories. For instance, his main theme can be said to be the abolition of exploitation on the workers in the corporate environment but he exploited, when he had a chance, the working people he happened to have a contact with. His peers looked at him as a boor because he behaved in an overbearing manner; however, they tolerated him, considering him to be a genius. He revealed, contrary to his intent, this true character of his in many parts of his *Capital*, though its presentation was scholarly throughout.

I would say that it was sheer madness to try to build a society based on such a poor and incomplete ideology. It is a surprise to me that it had taken more than 70 years after the Bolshevik Revolution before the Russian people realised they could not carry on the business of communism any more. In the Russian Empire under communist control, the brute force had suppressed the social and ethnic conflicts, and as soon as it loosened the grips all the problems came to the fore for everyone to see in the 1990s (Grenville 1994, p. 10). The Russian communist regime failed for economic cause rather than military or political or any other causes. Ironically Marx preached that economics were the determining factor of all human activities and it was this aspect of his doctrine which brought down the communism in Russia. Marx was right at least on this point in the Russian context.

Many young people think that it is natural for them to do their best in establishing their careers within the society. They don't realise how repugnant the idea is for the social reformers who place the social welfare before the establishment of their careers.

Alexander Pushkin presents the negative or pessimistic outlook towards life through his verse novel *Eugene Onegin* (1833). I am sure it was his true life view, though he lived financially well-off life.

One verse says: Home life means one long string of dreary scenes (Pushkin 1995, p. 106). Another verse goes: In all this world what's more perverted than homes in which the wretched wife bemoans her worthless mate, deserted--alone both day and night through life; or where the husband, knowing truly her worth (yet cursing fate unduly), is always angry, sullen, mute--a coldly jealous, selfish brute (p. 89)! Another goes: This fragile life that hurries so! Its worthlessness needs no professing (p. 54). He sadly attacks the life and social institutions in the following passages:

Oh, blest who in his youth was tender;
And blest who ripened in his prime;
Who learned to bear, without surrender,
The chill of life with passing time;
Who never knew exotic visions,
Nor scorned the social mob's decisions;
Who was at twenty fop or swell,
And then at thirty, married well,
At fifty shed all obligations
For private and for other debts;
Who gained in turn, without regrets,
Great wealth and rank and reputation;
Of whom lifelong verdict ran:
'Old X is quite a splendid man'.
(p. 189)

I am going to expound further the two topics of the pre-Third Prophecy era, China's dynastic cycles, and exploitation, in an effort to highlight the real states of the societies in a concrete form before the speculated advent of the Third Prophecy in a social scale.

I have chosen China's dynastic cycles from history and elucidate it in Section 2. I would say that what happened in China in relation to dynastic changes typifies what TR Malthus (1766-1834) proposed in his book *An Essay on the Principle of Population* (1798).

I explain the population theory by Malthus next as a preparatory step to China's dynastic cycles. He argues in the above book that the population, when unchecked, increases in a geometrical ratio and the subsistence increases only in an arithmetical ratio. The population will always expand to the upper most to be checked only by famine, war and ill-health.

Malthus belonged, together with Adam Smith and David Ricardo, the latter of whom Malthus met in 1811 and became close friends, to the classical economists whose underlying conviction is the insistence of naturalism in all facets of life, thus in economic activities of their concern. Malthus did not advocate the state intervention to prevent the large deaths of human beings due to famine, disease and war which, he maintained, resulted from overpopulation. He thought it as a natural consequence of the human folly. He drew his conclusion from what he observed in the harsh life of his time.

Before the publication of *An Essay on the Principle of Population* by Malthus, the people were ignorant of the correlation between the procreation rate and the population. People procreated to the limit, resulting in the suffering of the people. However, Malthus was not the first person who had written about the population theories. In the traditional China the Chinese scholars knew that the fundamental cause of the dynastic cycles was the overpopulation. Also Stangeland, an American, published a book in 1904, expounding the population theories developed before Malthus. (Robbins 1998, p. 169) Malthus' theory gave support to the low wages, since the extra wages do not help the workers with more mouths to feed. If we interpret his theory, World Wars One and Two were necessary because they killed a huge number of people, irrespective of how the historians allocated as the possible causes of these wars.

The English economist and clergyman Thomas Robert Malthus propounded his population theory by publishing *An Essay on the Principle of Population* anonymously in 1798. Over the next 28 years he published four subsequent editions, and in 1830 he provided a synopsis *A Summary View of the Principle of Population.*

I discuss the topic of exploitation in Section 3 to reinforce my argument. The abolition of social exploitation is the central theme of Karl Marx's theses. Many writers throughout human history decried the exploitation of humans by other humans and expressed it in various ways.

Interestingly both of the above subjects, that is, dynastic cycles and exploitation, are still clearly in evidence in our daily life. However, the features in these fields of human activities will radically alter if the sufficient numbers of the population practise the teaching of the Third Prophecy. After the introduction of the new philosophy on a social scale, the population of a nation will be drastically reduced and the concept of the dynastic cycles will be observed only in the historical context. Also negligible exploitations will mark the new society. The eliminations of the current problems in the new society as I explain in the next chapter are another reason why I present these topics here.

Population Theory by Malthus

Malthus postulated that the causes of population and depopulation followed a certain law since the world began--one of the laws of nature. In the above law, he thought that the passions of sex, though strong at all times, were a given quantity through the ages. (Malthus 1970, p. 114)

The contraception within marriage began to win currency in England in the 1820s. A kind of condom had been used by the English and Scottish in the previous century for premarital and extramarital activities. (p. 26)

Malthus graduated from Jesus College, Cambridge, in 1788 in the discipline of mathematics as a Wrangle--equivalent to the first class honours. Hence he was fully numerate though he had a marked speech impediment. (p. 8) He was born to the family of eight children but raised only three in his marriage. Malthus argued in the following manner.

All plants and animals have the capacity of increasing their kinds in a geometrical progression if unchecked. The humans are no exception and the population tends to double itself every 25 years, if unchecked. (p. 18)

Subsistence increases only in an arithmetical ratio. The power of population is a lot greater than the power in the earth to produce subsistence for people. Since food is necessary for the life of people, the difficulty of obtaining food places a strong and consistent check on population. A large portion of mankind must feel the shortage of food. (p. 71)

He based his argument on the following mathematical definitions:

- The geometrical progression increases by multiplications; 1, 2, 4, 8, 16, 32, etc.

- The arithmetic progression increases by additions; 1, 2, 3, 4, 5, 6, etc.

(p. 20)

If the multiplying factor is made increasingly smaller than one, the geometrical progression becomes increasingly smaller but this is not what Malthus intended to convey.

Animals and plants increase in a geometrical progression and in case of plants the increase is far greater than that of humans if counted in the number of seeds. However, the production of food is, in reality, limited by the available land and it increases in an arithmetic progression. (p. 20)

Later economists argued that Malthus in fact based his theory on the law of diminishing returns. If the unused land is cultivated because of the population pressure, the harvest returns on these lands—not fertile, not well-watered and not close to the markets and so on—will be smaller compared with the lands already cultivated. If the population is further increased and more resources—labour, fertilisers and so forth—are expended, the harvest returns will be smaller compared with those of the previous harvests. The law of diminishing returns means that the marginal return becomes smaller for the marginal input as the input is gradually increased.

Corn countries are more populous than pasture countries, and rice countries more populous than corn countries (p. 117).

It is generally agreed that all new colonies settled in healthy countries, where there was plenty of room and food, increased the population in an astonishing speed helped by free or little cost land. Some of the colonies from the ancient Greece more than equalled their parent states in population and strength in no time. Also the European settlements in the new world bear ample testimony to the truth of the above remark. (p. 104)

It is well known that the states recover quickly the lost population through war, pestilence or the accidents of nature, since there are enough lands and food for the recovery (p. 107).

In the United States of America, since its settlements, there was ample room for expansion for the white settlers and it was established that the population doubled itself in every 25 years for a century and a half since its settlement (p. 74). It may be surprising but the effect of immigration seems to be negligible for the total increase of the population (p. 231).

The military heroes fought for their glory. However, the fundamental cause of emigration was a scarcity of food; the population expanded beyond the means of supporting it. (p. 84)

The immediate cause of the increase of the population is the excess of the births above the deaths. The immigration and emigration have little to do with the result. (p. 262)

Malthus wrote:

> The power of population being in every period so much superior, the increase of the human species can only be kept down to the level of the means of subsistence by the constant operation of the strong law of necessity, acting as a check upon the greater power (p. 21).

To limit the human population there are two checks, preventive and positive, operating:

Preventive Checks

The parents do not have children with the foresight of the difficulty attending the rearing of the family. This entails abstinence of marriage, delayed marriage, intercourse with birth prevention and abortion. This limits the birth rate.

Positive Checks

This mode increases the death rate. The positive checks to population are extremely varied, and include every cause, whether arising from vice or misery, which in any degree contributes to shorten the natural duration of human life. This entails, apart from malnutrition and unwholesome living, infanticides, common diseases, epidemics, wars, plagues and famines.

The preventive checks and positive checks to the population can be resolved into moral restraint, vice and misery (p. 29):

Moral Restraint
This refers to abstinence of or delayed marriage.

Vice
People find sexual outlet without having children through homosexuality, prostitution and abortion.

Misery
The standard of living will fall, disease and infant mortality increase, famine may break out, and freedom may be in danger. Political and economic instability may promote civil and foreign wars.

In the economically advanced countries in the recent years, the check to population is done not by restraint of marriage but by the spread of birth control.

Malthus posited that the overpopulated nations will suffer; and famine, plague and war will reduce their population. The Bible says:

> God will destroy the unfaithful people with the sword, i.e., by war, famine and plague (Jeremiah 14:12). Because of all the wicked and detestable practices of the house of Israel, they will fall by the sword, famine and plague (Ezekiel 6:11).

It is interesting to note that Malthus and the Bible postulate the depopulation of the people from the different sets of the premises. As a matter of fact people also tried to solve the problem of overpopulation by other means such as introduction of farming, industrialisation, emigration or human sacrifices. It has been conjectured that the emigration of the Caucasians from the steppes of southern Russia over two millenniums originated in the overpopulation. Also the vast scale human sacrifices in the Aztec culture may have been, conscious or subconscious on the part of the people, an attempt to reduce the surplus population. The educated people in the economically advanced countries today also generally advocate the population check by the practice of birth control.

Malthus raised only a small family. He thought it was a lot easier to bring in death control rather than birth control to the general population. (Malthus 1970, p. 46)

Famine is the first sign of the food shortage in a country and the other vices are to follow if the famine does not depopulate sufficiently (p. 118).

Famine has been a serious problem through the human history and has struck one region of the world every few years. The main cause of famine may be crop failures which result from drought, too much rainfall and flooding, plant diseases and pests. Possibly the weather has a great deal to do with even the plant diseases and pests. Many people in Africa, Asia and Latin America today are barely enough food at the best of times. It is said that a half billion people today are under-nourished.

Famines also lend to the easy spread of epidemics such as cholera and typhus, because not only people are malnourished but they are exposed to unhygienic conditions--dirty water and congregations of the fleeing people.

Malthus reasoned that it was wrong to bring in social amelioration, to decrease the infant mortality rate and to keep people healthy. These measures will increase the population and the overall situation will be worse. (p. 7)

Darwin wrote:

> I saw, on reading Malthus on *Population*, that natural selection was the inevitable result of the rapid increase of all organic beings (p. 50).

Alfred Russell Wallace, also credited with independently inventing the theory of evolution of species by natural selection, wrote after admitting that he got the inspiration from Malthus' *Principle of Population* which was perhaps the most important book he had read:

> Why do some die and live? And the answer was clearly, that on the whole the best fitted live. From the effects of disease the most healthy escaped; from enemies the strongest, the swiftest or the most cunning; from famine, the best hunters or those with the best digestion; and so on. Then it flashed upon me that this self-acting process would necessarily improve the race, because in every generation the inferior would inevitably be killed off and the superior would remain--that is, the fittest would survive. (p. 51)

Marx and Engels did not see any need to restrict the population growth and thought that the population theory Malthus developed undermined their production theory (p. 52). Particularly F Engels was a bitter critic of Malthus' theory (p. 35). However, Lenin insisted that the availability of both contraception and abortion be necessary conditions of human emancipation (p. 54).

Section 2 China's Dynastic Cycles

The introduction of farming in several parts of the world about 10 000 years ago enabled the same area to support more people and brought the increase of the population density. The last glacial period ended about 12 000 years ago and distinctly warmer climate dominated the globe ever since, though the earth scientists say that the globe is in the interglacial period at present and another ice age is on its way.

It is generally agreed that the world could support 5-10 million people before the agricultural revolution, that is, the introduction of farming. By the beginning of the Christian era, 8000 years after the introduction of farming, the human population was estimated to be 170 million. There was little population increase in the next 1000 years. By 1750, just before the Industrial Revolution in Britain, the world population may have been 800 million. This means that in the 750 years from 1000 to 1750, the annual population growth rate averaged only about one-tenth of one per cent. (*Encyclopaedia Britannica*, 15th edn, sv, Population.)

The spread of the Industrial Revolution which began in Britain in 1760 in the other parts of the world led to the huge increase of the world population:

In 1800, the world population reached 900 million;
in 1930, 2000 million;
in 1960, 3000 million;
in 1974, 4000 million;
in 1990, 5000 million.

The following description looked at from the individual life was referring to the North African situation in the modern context, but it is equally true to the bulk of the population the world over before the modern era. Sahel is a vast semi-arid region of North Africa, to the south of Sahara.

> Traditional life was never easy, and the hard fact of infant mortality served to limit the population. It was natural that a premium was placed on large families: children provided valuable labour and in later years, the only source of support their aging parents could count on. In time, advances in medical, sanitation and other areas brought about a gain in life expectancy, but the people of Sahel continued to have as many children as possible. (Ward 1989, p. 288)

In the past the following proposition was the norm anywhere in the world in the absence of the other indicators. The most decisive mark of the prosperity of any country is the increase of the number of the inhabitants, and the large population gave the sense of security from the aggression of the neighbouring countries.

When a country is prosperous, a large number of children were looked at as a source of opulence rather than a burden (Smith 1991, p. 74).

In any underdeveloped nations in the 20th century such as China, the birth rate remained high but the death rate was reduced dramatically with the aid of modern medicine. The above observation makes the pessimistic outlook for the future of the underdeveloped countries which make up two-thirds of the world population today (Dye, Moore & Holly 1996, pp. 11, 593). Any improvements, economic, sanitary or medicinal, are all absorbed by the extra population to feed, and become null after a while. It is estimated in 1999 that 97% of the baby births are in the Third World. China's prominence as the world power became apparent towards the end of the 20th century.

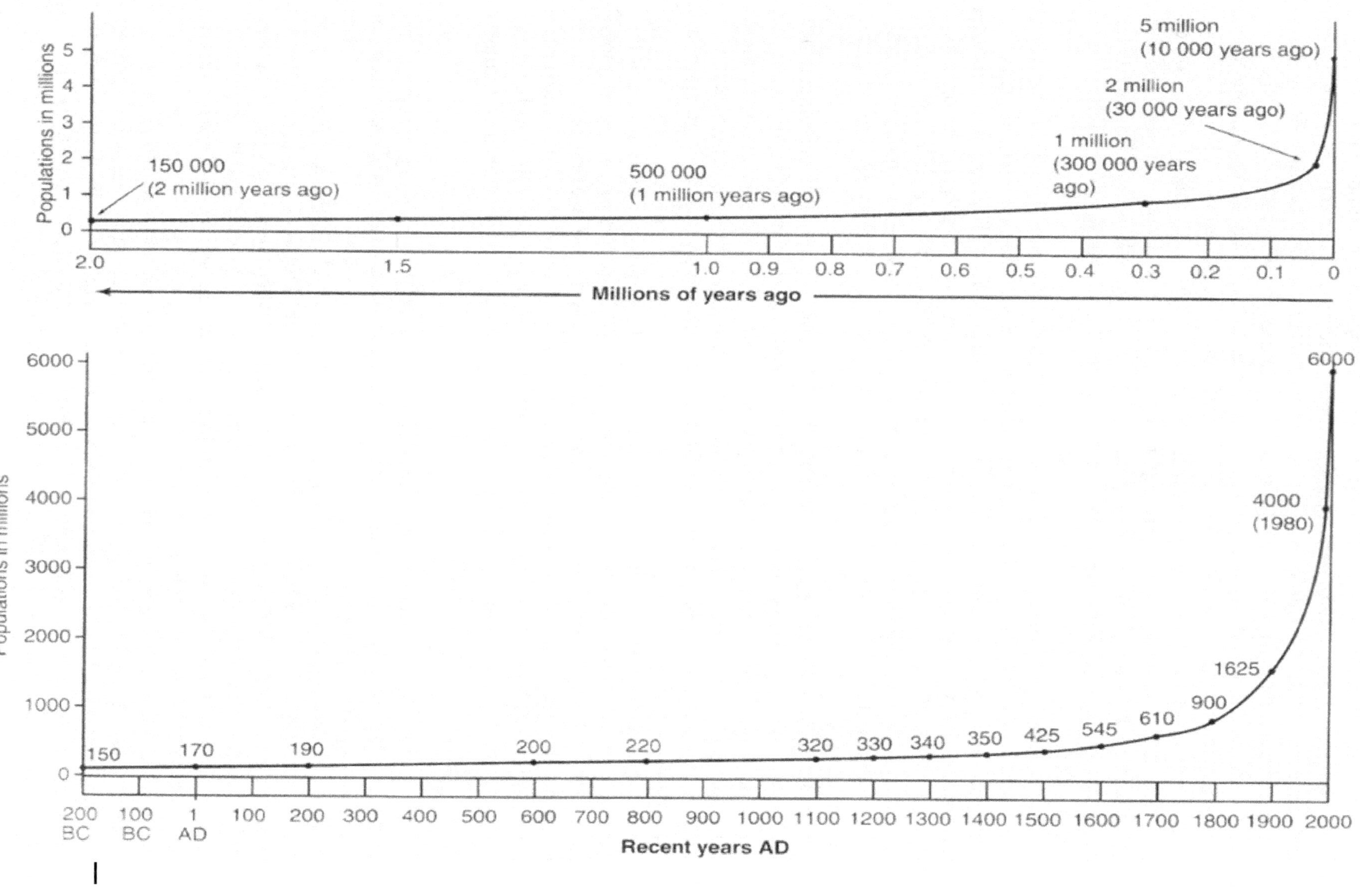

ILLUSTRATION 1 Human population growth in the Stone Age (top graph) and in recent centuries (bottom graph).
(Fig. 16.11 Sale, Colin, 1944, *Our wonderful world*, 2nd edn, Longman Cheshire, Melbourne.)

One of the striking features of Chinese civilisation may be said to be its continuity through centuries, overriding the dynastic changes. The fact that the essentially same Chinese characters have been used beyond the various dialects through the ages underpins not only symbolically but also practically the opening statement. The formal versions of written characters remained relatively stable since the script reform of the third century BC by the First Emperor (Shih huang-ti) to the twentieth century (Oliphant 1992, p. 176). Another outstanding feature of the continuity may be the system of the civil service examinations to man the bureaucracy. Refer to Introduction to Series, Book One, for details. China experienced changes of dynasties (ruling families) in a similar fashion to those of any other civilisations but the dynastic changes were superimposed on the continuous civil life of China proper. Dynastic cycles literally mean the repeated changeover of ruling families but the term is especially fitting to and discernible in the Chinese context, as I will disclose in the subsequent analyses.

The dynasty around the world referred to the family, though the bondage of the family was not only blood relation but marriage and adoption as we normally understand today. Further, the following considerations at times played the crucial role. The appointment of the new ruler could be based on tradition, the express will of the deceased ruler or the decision of the ruling advisory body. China and Europe as for many other kingdoms or empires of the world operated on the above pattern; however, each transition was different and we do not know how it happened or if it was peaceful or violent (family feuds or armed conflicts) until we examine each case.

The Roman Empire may deviate considerably from the above general rule: Because of its republican origin and its social system, the army and Senate, apart from the family connections, played a prominent role in deciding the successor issue. In the first place the Roman law recognised adoption as the same as kinship, and many emperors adopted a capable man to succeed him. Also the army and Senate at times appointed the successor to the dead or deposed emperor.

However the new ruler was appointed, it is strange to note that the running of kingdoms and empires depended on the family; and kings or queens and emperors or empresses looked at their domains as their properties until the modern democratic system was introduced. These rulers thought they could trust their family members most and conducted their business in an effort to preserve them, in much the same way the rich people carry out their business today. Thus the social convention more of less decided on the successor from the reigning dynasty.

Dynastic (of family) rule governed empires and kingdoms through the history in many parts of the world. The family affairs were played out with the various characters of the successors such as competency and popularity.

At the death of the reigning monarch, challengers may appear claiming they are the legitimate successors or from the various other reasons. These claimants can appear even while the monarch is on the throne. The appointed officials in the reigning government are more likely to follow the conventional successor thinking that they could secure the same position. The general public also tend to support the conventional successor thinking that there will not be any unrests or armed conflicts.

Elizabeth I was Elizabeth Tudor and James I was James Stuart, and Nicholas II was Nicholas Romanov, clearly indicating the royal house (surname or family name). Napoleon was his personal name; his family name was Bonaparte. To make the distinctions among the same family name, for example, Napoleon I, Napoleon II and Napoleon III were used. Elizabeth I was of Tudor family, and Elizabeth II is of Windsor family though King George

V changed the British royal family from the German Saxe-Coburg and Gotha to the above English name due to the anti-German sentiment during World War I.

The ruling families of the day controlled the Chinese dynasties though some dynasties were governed by the foreigners and referred to the Mongol dynasty or Manchu dynasty. The titles of the Chinese dynasties as we know can be the royal house name such as Chou, Ch'in, Sui, Han and T'ang, or the regional state name. The regional state before conquering most of China could have taken its name from the region or the ruling house or even the factional name and it is hard for us to ascertain until we make a research. A rebel general (Zhao Kuangyin to become Emperor Sung Taizu) started the Sung dynasty. Ming Hongwu, having arisen from a rebel peasant, established the Ming (meaning bright) dynasty. It seems that the foreign conquerors used Chinese names Yuan (Great Origin) instead of Mongol and Ch'ing or Qing (both meaning clear) instead of Manchu in consideration for the sensitivity to the Chinese people. All in all we should not place too much significance to the naming of the dynasties.

The Chinese civilisation of today is without any doubt the descendant of the Shang dynasty which made an appearance in the alluvial plain of the Yellow River in 1700s BC. In this sense China, as for Egypt, has the longest lasting civilisation in the world. (Whitehouse & Wilkins 1986, p. 18)

Thinkers were divided between holders of the cyclic view and holders of one-way view of time. These different views of time have consequent different views of human history and life. The cyclic view of history, both cosmic and human, has been prevalent among the Hindus, the Greeks, the Chinese and the Aztecs. The order and disorder in Chinese and Egyptian history reinforce the cyclic view. Dynastic cycles further lead to civilisation cycles.

In Hindu tradition, cosmic time ended up by imposing the idea of circular time and cosmic cycle. Cosmic cycle denotes the infinite repetition of the same rhythm of birth, death and rebirth. In post Vedic India, this conception developed into two intertwined doctrines: that of cycles repeated to infinity and that of transmigration of souls. (Eliade 1978, p. 42)

Dynastic cycles, philosophically speaking, come from the concept that the event repeats itself in many cycles.

If we study the history of China and Europe, we get the impression that China tended to be cyclic in progress and emotional in character, whereas Europe tended to be progressive in a straight line and analytical in their approach to life. China is feminine and Europe is masculine. China was more advanced in many measures than Europe in the pre-modern era in the same way the girls are more advanced in many measures than the boys before adolescence. Europe became decidedly superior to China in the modern context in a similar way the boys become decidedly superior to the girls after adolescence.

The doctrine of returning to the original is prominent in Lao-tzu. It has contributed in no small degree to the common Chinese cyclical concept, which teaches that both history and reality operate in cycles. The cycles appear not only as days, seasons and years but in human happiness, events and history. It is often said that history repeats itself.

The life views of Confucius, Mencius and Lao-tzu were all idealistic, disregarding material culture, sex and race. Dynastic cycles may connote that the history repeated itself without progress. That connotation may be justified in idealism which appears that China did not make a significant progress since the Warring Period (475-221 BC). However, that view is definitely incorrect for the Chinese society as a whole if we look at the materialistic advancement of the Chinese society through the ages. Dynastic cycles fundamentally denote the expansion and contraction of the population accompanied by the changes of dynasties, and refer to any accompanying changes.

We are here concerned with underlying causes of change of authority rather than the specific dynastic changeover to the next. However, under the heading of Modern China later in this section, I give out some detailed information on the transition from the Manchu (Ch'ing) dynasty (the last of the imperial dynasty in China) to the communist rule. I treat the development of communism in China in Section 3, Chapter 1, Book 3 *Communism*. The transition not only gave a sharp break from the past but it was done for the sake of communism. However, I present the narration to emphasise that the changeover was fundamentally a dynastic cycle. Mao Zedong was not the first man who had proposed the land distribution among the landless peasants. The hunger for the ownership of the lands had been acutely strong in the rural areas not only in China but the world over. Many people, for example, the Taipings, used the idea to challenge the governing authority. Mao himself thought he was an emperor after the establishment of the People's Republic of China in 1949 and behaved like one, though he established a republic not an empire. I detail this aspect of his life focusing on his sexual exploits in Section 15, Chapter 1, Book 5 *The Sexual Laws*.

Broadly speaking, the fundamental need to transform, Chinese and non-Chinese, some scholars allege, was the overpopulation with the limited cultivated land which supplied limited food. Lack of food for everyone in the society forced the removal of the top echelon of the ruling class which were ultimately responsible for feeding all the people under their care. The challengers were risking their lives and only when the society was extremely disorderly they went ahead with the challenge. Subsequently the victors (with battles or trickery) appointed the new or incumbent officials as it suited them. Another ruling family replaced this ruling family when the overpopulation forced the changeover in the next round of the cycle.

There is an abundance of Chinese historical writings how the specific dynasty gave way to the new dynasty. The basic plot may be stated as follows:

> The Son of Heaven (Emperor) of the ruling dynasty angers people and hence Heaven by his corrupt conducts. For example, King Chow, last king of the Shang dynasty, was known to be utterly wicked. A good man comes forward and deposes the reigning emperor by trickery or armed conflicts. If people have confidence in the victor, he becomes an emperor with the Mandate of Heaven, thus inaugurating a new dynasty. The narration centres on the moral degradation of the vanquished ruler and on the high ethical level of the new ruler rather than the political and economic policies, being similar to the narrations in the Christian Bible.

Personally I don't see any difference between Heaven in China; and God or Lord of the Bible. The Son of God or the Son of the Most High refers to Jesus Christ in the New Testament (e.g., Luke 1:32, 35; John 1:34). Son of man in the Old Testament as is often used in Ezekiel is a poetic synonym for man. Jesus Christ used the term to refer to himself, possibly meaning a Messiah as the book of Daniel makes the first reference to the Messiah as the Son of Man (Daniel 7:13). These designations are figures of speech, probably metaphors.

The new emperor's claim to the new dynasty stands on primarily virtue and secondarily ability. The rebel leader can defeat the incumbent emperor only when he is capable militarily and politically; however, the Chinese literature always emphasises the high moral ground of the victorious emperor whose ability came from his virtue. The subsequent emperor is deemed fit to rule because he is the highest ranking son in the ruling family: virtue and ability are there only by chance. The new emperor receives the Mandate of Heaven and thus carries out the command of Heaven. The Mandate of Heaven is the divine authority to rule and not the result of democratic votes. In the West the divine right of a king has often been touted through history in contrast with democracy (Harris 1999, p. 122).

The emperors and their subjects of the various social levels traditionally performed the veneration for ancestors in China. The emperors worshipped Heaven with zeal. The Confucian tradition emphasised the reverence for ancestors, the cult of classics and the fixed social order. The merchants tended to disrupt the above tradition, which was one basic reason why the Confucians disliked the merchants. (p. 125)

The Duke of Zhou (Chou) conquered the last Shang king in ca. 1028 BC. In the famous proclamation, the former justified his revolt against the king by the order he had received from the Celestial Lord to put an end to a corrupt and odious domination. This is the first statement of the famous doctrine of the 'Heavenly Mandate'. (Eliade 1982, p. 9)

Heaven is conceived as divine, semi-natural, semi-personal force, and similar in many ways to God of the Old Testament. The anthropomorphic God of the Old Testament is quite different from the omniscient and omnipotent God of the New Testament. The following passage is from the Chinese source but reminds us of the Old Testament:

> Heaven demonstrates its approval of an emperor by vouchsafing plentiful harvests, social order and portents of nature that are interpreted positively. Heaven manifests its displeasure with an emperor by sending down famine, drought, widespread sickness, political turmoil or other portents. (Lopez 1996, p. 29)

Traditional Chinese wisdom equated the Mandate of Heaven with the will of people as the following verses illustrate:

> Heaven sees with the eyes of the people.
> Heaven hears with the ears of people.
> (Sharma 1993, p. 97)

The emperors governed to make people happy. Good policies led to happy people and bad policies led to unhappy people. We can look at this idea as the basis of democracy. The Old Testament does not stand on democracy: The instructions to act not only in the moral issues but in political decisions came from the prophets who professed that they heard the words of God. Modern democracy is based on the number of people who approve the ruling body by voting.

Even Mencius, 'who like Confucius, lived in a period of political struggle, moral chaos and intellectual conflicts' (Chan 1963, p. 49), supported what we call the Chinese Constitution which expressly call for the rebellion against wicked rulers and their replacement. This constitution sounds like a justified homicide of the present age--but in the national scale. Mencius is known for his belief that human nature is good. He believed that the people of a nation had the right to depose or kill a bad ruler. A bad ruler was one who ignored the people's welfare and governed unkindly.

Mencius' idea is similar to the concept of the social contract between the ruler and the ruled. Jean Jacques Rousseau and John Locke supported the right to revolt against the incompetent government using the political theory of the social contract in the modern setting.

It is interesting to compare the qualities of the good or bad rulers from the Chinese and the biblical sources. The following listings remind us of the applicants' qualities required for the advertised positions in today's job vacancies.

The qualities of good rulers from the Chinese sources are:

> solemn, illustrious, sincere, correct, discriminating, pure, kind and affable (p. 11)

The qualities of bad rulers from the Chinese sources are:

> greedy, reckless, depraved, perverted, lewd, indolent, negligent, lazy, vulgar and cruel (p. 11)

The ways of the king from the biblical sources:

> Even so, he must not acquire many horses for himself, or return the people to Egypt in order to acquire more horses, since the Lord has said to you, 'You must never return that way again'. And he must not acquire many wives for himself, or else his heart will turn away; also silver and gold he must not acquire in great quantity for himself. (Deuteronomy 17:16-7)

Chinese people developed a foolproof theory that in a life and death struggle among the contestants (individuals, groups or nations), it is the victor whom Heaven favours: thus the way of Heaven is always right in supporting the victor. This corresponds to the Judaic faith that God does not make a mistake in judging an individual, a group or a nation. When I heard the above Chinese proposition the first time, I thought the idea to be quite strange and even ridiculous. It is not really strange after all, since we have no way of knowing who is morally right or militarily strong among the competitors until the result is out. The winner is sanctioned by Heaven in Chinese terms and by God in Jewish terms virtually by definition. Thus we can see remarkable parallels in the above setup, not only in that the judgement criteria of the rise and fall of the contestants are presence and absence of faith in Heaven or God and the accompanying ethical level but also in that the party Heaven or God favours always win in the end. We can also find many examples in the popular novels in that the author makes sure that the good guys always win in the end. In the Old Testament the favoured party is, individually, the most faithful persons; nationally the Hebrews, chosen people, still depending on their faith.

Why Was Ethics Emphasised in Various Conflicts in China and the Levant?

As the Jews did with the history in the Old Testament, the Chinese regarded history as important containing the moral and educational values, and left vast amount of historical writings, official and unofficial. Also the idea that Heaven gives a mandate to govern to a virtuous leader has been an important base of the Chinese political thinking. According to the oldest Chinese writing, the Duke of Zhou (Chou), thought to be a model ruler at the early Zhou period (1122-771 BC), made a statement in about 1120 BC that Hsia and Shang had to give way to Shang and Zhou respectively because their last kings were morally degenerate.

Readers may well think it odd that the judging criteria on the rulers are primarily their ethical levels both in China and the Levant. There are many justifiable reasons for this. The central theme of Judaism is the faith in the All-Mighty and not in the ethical teaching. However, I developed the following argument on the assumption that the faithful people are morally high and practically it is hard to make distinctions between the two manifestations.

In the ancient times in China as well as in the Levant, the authors of the records had to rely on the judgement criteria available to them such as the moral standards or motivations of the contestants when narrating an event in the absence of political and economic information. The general public believed that there was an unalienable correlation between the moral levels and the policies of the monarchs. Thus the monarchs were judged by the ethical standard. The successive imperial policy on the civil service examinations in China endorsed and strengthened the general thrust of the above judgement. The Manchu (Ch'ing) government (1644-1912), the last of the imperial dynasty in China, abolished the examination system in 1905, established modern school and sent students abroad to study. The other side of the coin of abolishing the examination system was that the Western knowledge was spreading to be used in the Chinese society, and people did not have to rely on the moral teachings of Confucius to carry on the business of governing. The scholars of later era came to stress political and economic forces rather than the individual integrity in explaining social phenomena because the social data were increasingly available to them. (Spielvogel 1991, p. 410) We today have sophisticated media such as newspapers, televisions, magazines and books, apart from specialised professional people, and it is hard for us to envision the informational environment the pre-modern authors were submerged.

There is another economic and practical reason why the pre-modern authors stressed the moral levels and motivations of the individuals. In the pre-industrial era all over the world, the economy was predominantly agricultural with the absence of significant industry. Certainly the industry, mining and trade were the sources of wealth; however, the wealth thus created flowed to the industrialists, the merchants, the land owners and the states, not to the farmers. Besides the wealth generated thus was small compared with the vast amount of wealth the agriculture created before the modern era. The national prosperity very much depended on the yields of crops and animals which were in turn largely dependent on weather with both the given quantity of land and the given quality of soil. The output of virtually every agricultural product is subject to unpredictable fluctuations of weather conditions--hours of sunshine, the amount of rainfall and the average temperature at the right season (McTaggart, Findley & Parkin 1992, p. 113).

Apart from the weather, there were other factors which influenced the prosperity of the farmers hence of the nations. It was important to select the right crops for the soil and weather and also for the demands of the people. The locations of the farming lands in relation to the consuming and labour markets were important. The irrigation system in place had also strong influence on the amount of the produce. Fertiliser and labour expended would have made a considerable difference on the amount to be harvested. However, in the overall assessment, provided the farmers did best to make the right decisions with the available resources--we have no reason to believe otherwise since their life depended on them, the weather had a vital influence on the amount of the crops they harvested under the given conditions. Karl Marx asserts that the amount of the crops depends on the accident of nature (Marx 1968, p. 221), though he emphasises the quality of soil and money invested for good harvests in the other parts of his works.

The ancient Greeks imagined that their gods lived in Mount Olympus, the highest mountain in Greece, and Zeus, the supreme God, was the sky god. They recognised the sky as vitally important, controlling the weather and hence the amount of crops and even their life and death. The Bible says that God is in Heaven. Similarly Confucian doctrines often say that Heaven controls the human fate.

There are other complications for the farmers. The farmers need a long period (weeks, months and even years) for the grains, fruits, cattle or timber to be ready for the markets. The farmers are dependent on weather for good harvests but also on the grain prices for their income arising from the produce. Good harvests in a large area may lower the grain prices and hence their disposable income. (Grenville 1994, p. 48) When poor harvests result in a large area, some farmers who harvested a large amount of crops escaping the damage by chance got extra income from the raised prices as it is today. The same argument holds true for the cattle production over a few years rather than shorter (yearly or less) period for the grains. Hence it was the norm the world over that the farmers were doomed to the subsistence living whatever they did. Karl Marx makes note of the constant poverty of the agricultural population in contrast to the progressive enrichment of the artisans (Marx 1963, p. 68). Also the ruling class wanted the farmers in no-win situation such that they themselves could lead the comfortable life, extracting heavy taxes and rents, and labour from the farmers. As far as I know the good life of the farmers was exception to the general rule of the hard life everywhere in the world through the human history.

The ruling class as a rule not only occupied the important government posts but owned large tracts of farm lands. In the pre-modern society people had strong attachment to the farm lands as the source of wealth. In contrast people in the modern society look at lands, houses, businesses, professions, investments or any other valuables as the source of wealth.

The farmers were also easy targets of the government policies. They were scattered all over the country with poor communications and high illiteracy. Before the introduction of the democratic system in the modern era, they could not even voice their disapproval by voting. Besides a large number of farmers produced a large amount of tax collected and the burden on each farmer was comparatively small, that is, the tax was broad based.

The fact that the peasants lived on the subsistence level everywhere was not the purpose but only the means by which the elite of the society could lead a comfortable life. The peasants here as used rented or owned a small piece of land and were also called peasant farmers. The social system backed by the army allowed the crops, labour and money to flow from the peasants to the upper class in the concrete forms of the law, that is, taxes, rent on the farm lands and corvèe. The top echelon of the elite, kings or emperors, promulgated the laws, if not the social customs, such that the greatest shares fell upon them, and the other upper class got benefits in proportion to their social hierarchy in exchange for supporting the social system. The laws also made sure that the peasants were bound to the farms and did not run away looking for a better life: the peasants were needed in the farms to produce the crops and cattle with little gains. In addition the floods and droughts brought tremendous suffering to the peasants who formed the bulk of the population the world over before the Industrial Revolution of Britain in the 18th century and subsequent industrialisation in the other parts of the world: many of them had to die by starvation. There was not even the weather forecast people could rely on. Women in China in general as in any other parts of the world were fated to subservient to men in sexual terms and many other ways.

The above system was the general pattern of the world before the modern democracy was introduced. It was practically impossible to deviate from the set rule from the various reasons already mentioned. Let's look at the reign of Catherine the Great (1729-96) of Russia as an example. She initiated her reign enthusiastically with the spirit of Enlightenment. Towards the end of her rule the idea of Enlightenment disappeared from her policies. Ironically she brought the zenith of serfdom in Russia, in order to bind the noble and gentry class to her. Section 15, Chapter 1, Book Five *The Sexual Laws* gives out further information focusing on her sexual exploits.

The agriculture was by far the greatest economic sector in each term of labour and capital, often 90% is quoted, in the pre-industrial nations all over the world. The bulk of the population had hardly enough food to eat even at the best of times because of taxes, rents on the farm lands and widespread corvèe system. In the early 20th century in China 50 to 70% of the crops was charged as a rent. Chiang Kai-shek tried to lower it to 37%; however, without success as for many of his reforms (Milston 1978, p. 316). It was common in Britain in the 18th century that the agricultural rent was one-third of the gross produce (Marx 1968, p. 363). It was also a common practice in Europe before capitalism that the peasants, [who did not own the land they cultivated], carried out corvèe-labour, two days a week, in addition to rent, for the landlord whether it may be a private person or the state (Marx 1959, p. 794). Under these circumstances the government policies hardly mattered. The governing bodies could have initiated the irrigations system for farming and opened the canals and roads to facilitate the transport of food and people: the implementation of these measures needed more taxes. The landowners did not pay rents; however, the history showed that a large number of small landholders had to pay heavy taxes and only a small number of the large landowners escaped heavy taxes using their influence. Even in the present sophisticated society the government is noted for inefficiency the world over, and we can imagine what the government was like in the pre-industrial and inefficient society. The good measures undertaken counted little if the bad weather lasted for many years. Overall the weather, not the government policies, decided the fortunes of the nations. Hence, the authors looked for the moral standards of the rulers rather than their policies on the assumption that the rulers with high integrity would possess good judgement and deliver good policies.

I shall give an example. The Old Testament refers to the bad harvests in the Levant as the reason why the Israelites, Jacob and his offspring, moved to Egypt in search for food but does not mention anything about the policies in the Levant. Pharaoh's policy to store the grains collected during the years of the good harvests does not make much sense to us except in the sense that it banned the export of grains from Egypt. The Bible does not explain why people in the Levant did not take the same measure after the good harvests if they had at all. (Genesis 41-6)

In the pre-industrial society all over the world the weather decided not only the prosperity or decline of the society but life or death of many of the inhabitants. Hence the wish for good weather and harvests was shown in the human sacrifices. HG Wells wrote that human sacrifices were carried out at the sowing season in many parts of the world, praying for the good weather. However, there is definite evidence in many other parts of the world to support the reasons for human sacrifices other than wishing for good harvests. The human beings such as concubines, servants and guards were sacrificed to accompany the important dead persons in China. As time went on the pottery figures were substituted. (Harris 1999, p. 147) Under the Zhou era, human sacrifices were replaced by wooden or terracotta figures, with which the tomb of Shih huang-ti of Ch'in in later era was protected (p. 106).

Apart from the above scenarios, the scholars proposed a theory explaining the underlying cause of dynastic changes in China, which is our main topic of this section. China proper as idealistically ruled by an emperor had limited land: the frontier of agricultural lands had virtually ceased as early as the Han dynasty (206 BC-AD 221). The land mass available for the production of food did not increase by substantial amount since then to the present--for two millenniums. Though the historians in the ancient China recorded agricultural land shortage as early as the fourth century BC, the problem did not become serious until around 100 BC during the Han period. 'The Chinese population grew rapidly in the Former Han period; the census of AD 2 recorded a population of fifty-eight million, making the Han Empire somewhat more populous that the contemporaneous Roman Empire.' (Ebrey 1996, p. 73) This assessment does not mean that the Chinese population remained static since the Han period. The more manpower expended on agriculture resulted in more harvests of crops and cattle from the same acreage. This was particularly pronounced for rice, whose relationship, that is, more rice from more labour, is a prominent economic feature observable even today. As the farming technique improved, the greater harvests naturally resulted. Also more arable lands, though limited in scope, were opened for the production of food. Because of these reasons, China was capable of feeding more mouths as the time went on.

The late T'ang (618-907) political fragmentations so lamented by political thinkers seem, if anything, to have stimulated economic growth. One of the clearest signs of this is the doubling of the population between 750 and 1100. In 742 China's population was still approximately 50 million, the same as it had been in AD 2. Over the next three centuries with the expansion of rice cultivation in central and southern China, China's food supply steadily increased and so did the population, which reached 100 million by 1100. (p. 141)

> Dynastic decline came inexorably to the Ming (1368-1644), as it had come to all previous ruling houses. The pattern was a familiar one: reign by weak and self-indulgent emperors, official corruption and bureaucratic factionalism, abuse of power by court eunuchs (a particularly acute problem during the Ming dynasty), fiscal irresponsibility, neglect of

> public works, natural disasters and the rise of rebellion. (Murowchick 1994, p. 157)

Why didn't the dynastic cycles perpetuate in the Western Roman Empire in the way as it did in the Chinese empires? The dynastic changes occurred in both of these empires (the dynasty meant basically families) probably as for any other empires and kingdoms. However, the setups of these two empires were quite different. It is true, for example, that the Roman emperors were chosen from the Julio-Claudian dynasty until AD 68; they were the relatives of Augustus, the first Roman Emperor. There was no suggestion that the termination of the Julio-Claudian dynasty was caused by overpopulation as for any other dynasties of the Western Empire and even in the Eastern Empire. There was a strong tradition that the reigning emperors adopted capable men, instead of their blood relatives, to succeed them. Also a large number of the reigning emperors were murdered. Quite often the dubious claimants were recognised as emperors. These features characterised the Western Empire through its life. Succeeding emperors with their strong personalities and shrewd judgements needed the support of the army, the Senate and the people. It is said that as time went on the emperor's power increased in the Western Empire and the people became less active politically, which is said to be the indication of the decline of the empire.

I am to present the following views of mine without the documental evidence. The Roman frontiers with huge mileage were open and the people moved away from the overpopulated region which had consequent difficulties. Further the empire was perpetually engaged in wars which reduced the population. It may be that the Roman Empire as a whole was underpopulated through the ancient and classical periods. The perennial expansion drive of the empire did not originate in the overpopulation.

In Europe, the upper limit of the population did not reach until around the year 1300: the European continent could not support substantially more population with the available lands and contemporary farming techniques. The population as a whole, if exceeded the upper limit, were undernourished or some had to starve to death. In fact, one major cause of easy spread of the Black Death since the 14th century was attributed to the malnutrition of the bulk of the Europeans. (Spielvogel 1991, p. 367) They had to wait for the Industrial Revolution of the 18th century both for the improvements of the agricultural techniques to increase the outputs and subsequent trade expansion to import food, and consequently to lift substantially the number of supportable population.

In the modern era the similar story unfolds. The Spanish Flue of 1918-9 killed more than 20 million people, young and old, of virtually all the nations on earth. The cause is attributed to the undernourishment of people as the result of World War One. Ten million people are said to have died as the direct result of the war.

During the Industrial Revolution in Britain, 'productivity per man, output per head and total output rose in agriculture'. Thus Britain did not have to import a large quantity of food in spite of sharply increased population since the middle of the 18th century. 'Only in years of bad harvest were mass food imports necessary.' (Mathias 1969, p. 67)

Adolf Hitler wrote the following passage in Munich just before World War One:

> Germany has an annual increase of population of nearly nine hundred thousand souls. The difficulty of feeding this army of new citizens must grow greater from year to year and ultimately end in catastrophe unless ways and means are found to forestall the danger of starvation and misery in time. (Hitler 1992, p. 120)

However, the following reasoning reflected Hitler's true position on overpopulation. The overpopulations among the neighbouring nations would result in serious struggles for existence. Only the fittest nation, hopefully Germany he reasoned, would survive as a dominant nation. He saw the above selection process as good and he objected to the population restriction and also proposed early marriage for young men, stating primarily to prevent the spread of syphilis. He had observed at first hand the ill effect of this venereal disease in the German army. Possibly he did not know that early marriage would result in the large family and hence statistically would end up creating a populous nation.

Another twist to his population theory was that he did not practise what he preached. He was childless and married his lover just before their deaths.

Data - Population

China's Population Growth, A.D. 0 - 2050

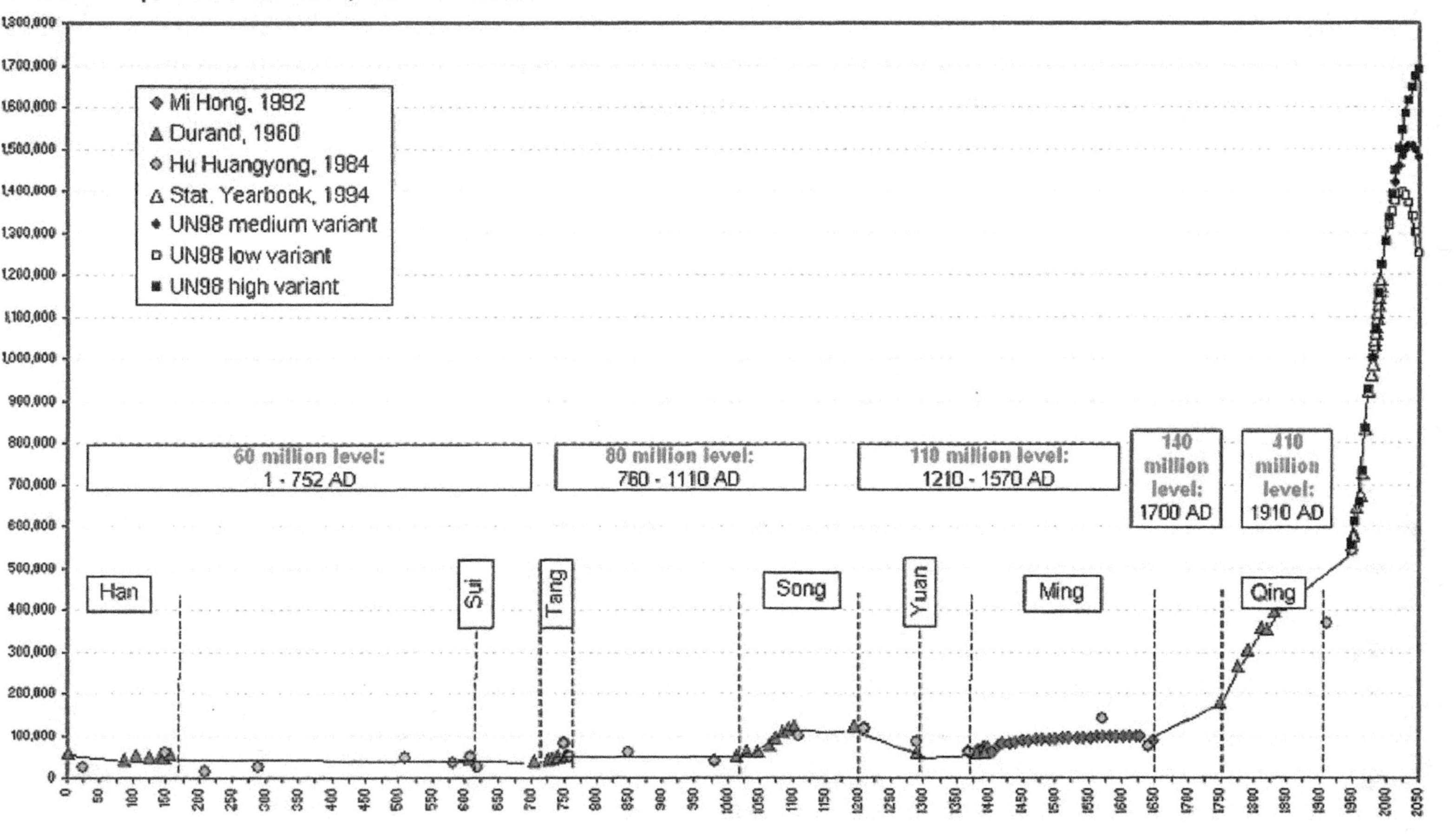

ILLUSTRATION II

I stated earlier in this section that the agricultural land shortage was not a serious consideration in China until around 100 BC, during the Han period. The fact that there were the Hsia, Shang, Zhou and Ch'in dynasties in China before the Han dynasty seems to tell us convincingly that the land shortage is not the only cause of dynastic turnover. However, we have to take into account the following facts. Hsia, Shang and Zhou were all local dynasties and did not cover China as we know today. The land shortage practically means the cultivated lands within the civilised regions. The spare lands outside the regions and even inside the regions if uncultivated did not produce any food. Although the Zhou era lasted nearly 800 years from about 1000 BC to 221 BC, some of which were only nominal. The Ch'in dynasty ruled over China as an empire but lasted for less than 20 years, from 221 BC to 206 BC: the termination was not due to the overpopulation. The foregoing views, also, do not take into account the poor harvests of crops because of floods and droughts which must have happened quite often. Even in our present age of high technical levels, we often hear of bumper or poor harvests which primarily depend on weather. The poor harvest of a particular region in the classical to medieval China was felt severely by the local people by virtue of lack of communications and transports: the unimportant people ultimately paid with their lives, as is normally the case even today that the unimportant people suffer as the results of various misfortunes or calamities. Unimportant people are often expressed as people in the lower strata of the society or insignificant people or little people. In the French Revolution and the 20th century communist revolutions, the mobs attacked the elite by the natures of the revolutions. But these were exceptions to the general rule of the societies in the overall development of the long human history.

Drought, torrential rains, high winds and insects can wipe out the crops, though the crop damages from these causes originating in the freak weather are mostly regional. For example, in the United States as a whole between 1929 and 1939, the crop harvest figures showed remarkable stability, in spite of a large number of crop failures which must have been reported during the 10 year period, as they are today. We are referring to the nations with the huge land mass, such as China and the USA, covering roughly the same area. The drought that gripped Australia in the years 2002-10 virtually covered the whole continent. Australia is known as a dry continent and the above drought is said to be the worst since the records started more than one hundred years earlier.

The crop failures in such vast countries as China and the USA can be assumed to be always regional. But the famine of 1958-63 in China was caused by the policy failures and was state-wide. It is said that this famine was the worst in the world history and over 30 million Chinese died as a consequence.

The First Emperor (also called Shih huang-ti) of Ch'in would have been aware of serious food shortage that might arise in the future, to be accompanied by the destruction of his dynasty. He employed a vast number of people in harsh working conditions for the phenomenal constructions of such as the Great Wall of China, 270 palaces at Afang, his mausoleum at Mount Li, the Royal Roads, the canals and irrigation systems. The Great Wall, which is familiar to us all and on which particularly harsh working conditions were applied, was installed obviously to ward off the foreign invaders. At the same time it marks the limit of the settled agriculture, thus the Chinese civilisation: the lay of the wall lies approximately on the 380 mm isohyet (Cotterell & Morgan 1975, p. 50). The Great Wall, when properly defended, was a bulwark against the nomadic peoples in the north. This did not mean the same to the Chinese. About AD 100, the Han armies conquered land north of the Great Wall and the Chinese went beyond the wall for habitation whenever they felt the pressure of the overpopulation within the wall, whose facts are contrary to the foregoing assertions.

One of the major reasons behind these huge projects was probably to kill off a large population which became redundant since the cessation of the unification wars in 221 BC. The state of Ch'in engaged in 15 major campaigns between 364 BC and 234 BC, and the number of casualties among the enemy states alone was placed at 1.5 million in *Shih-chi* by Ssu-ma Ch'ien. *Shih-chi*, which is the major source of information about Shih huang-ti, does not refer to the emperor's intent to eliminate a large number of people in the hope to stabilise his empire. Men not women were killed by wars and harsh working conditions at the various construction sites. Upon reflection it would have been more effective to kill women to reduce the population. However, Shih huang-ti may not have had this knowledge and besides the wars and constructions were necessary to satisfy his personal ego. The population of China at that time was estimated to be 40 million. (Guisso & Pagani 1989, p. 31)

In this light, the emperor showed a remarkable foresight concerning the population and the stability of his empire. If the foregoing assessment is correct, not only must he have believed that the fundamental cause of dynastic change was overpopulation, but he put the theory into practice sacrificing a huge number of people.

The population at large could not stand the heavy burdens of taxes and corvèe (forced labour), and the Ch'in regime collapsed in 206 BC soon after the death of Shih huang-ti in 210 BC. Thus ironically, it is clear to us that the demise of Ch'in did not come about because of overpopulation but it collapsed because of one man's incredible determination to administer unified China for the benefits of its people and dynasty.

Through the course of Chinese history, the land was cleared continually for cultivation and pasteurisation with varying enthusiasm. However, the crop and cattle productions did not catch up with the rapid population growth. Malthus described this discrepancy as 'the food increases only in an arithmetic proportion but the population increases in a geometric proportion'.

At the time of poor harvests, the peasants did not normally have substantial savings; money or grains. They didn't often have resources to last till the next harvests. It may be argued that they should have prepared the uncultivated forests or arid lands which were available for them at the time of plenty. We have to consider a large manpower required to put into use the arable lands, apart from the agricultural implements and seeds. It took months before the cleared lands started producing a sizable quantity of crops. A huge manpower to clear the lands, saving of the seeds, planting and looking after them, and months of waiting for the harvests, and also some chance that all the efforts may not pay off in the end--another bad weather, stealing of the crops by the marauders, and the confiscation of the crops by the government officials. All these must be taken into account, which the peasants may not be willing to take because of the immediate needs for the food even at the time of supposed plenty. Understandably, the hungry peasants at the poor harvest opted for desperate measures rather than patiently waiting for the food to be produced from their land or the newly opened lands. We may find the analogy in the students' unwillingness to study intensely until just before the important examinations, though time and again they feel they must be prepared long before the examinations.

The import of food stuffs into China was quite limited not only because the Chinese general public were reluctant to rely on the neighbouring countries which they regarded as inferior as they still do today, but also because these countries would have had small surplus of grains if any at all. Even if the mandarins had recommended the importation of grains out of sheer necessity, the imperial pride would not have allowed it. (Loewe 1990, p. 269) The Chinese were conscious of Sino-centric notion that China was the centre of the world. The imperial court of whatever persuasions would have collapsed unless they upheld the notion in the official capacity. The famous Silk Road was for transportation of luxuries only such as silk, gold, jewellery and potteries, as we can easily ascertain from the vast distances involved and the small amount of merchandises transportable: the import of a large quantity of grains for profit motive was out of question through this route.

The peasants were on the subsistence economy, and the surplus crops and cattle they produced were taken away as tax or rent. It may be apt to say that tax and rent were fixed such that the peasants were not left with any surplus. As the population grew, the surplus of food became scarce in general terms. If the poor harvests because of the adverse weather lasted for a few years, the prices of food especially rice, since rice was the staple food in China in the similar way bread was the main staple in Europe, went through the roof. Many people, not being able to secure something to eat, naturally became desperate and risked everything including their lives in trying to obtain food. Whatever argument the government officials came up with as to the reason for the lack of food and whatever theories they came up with for solving the food shortage, the peasants were not interested in arguments and theories but had to have something to eat to survive. Thus the riots broke out and a large number of people, most of whom were peasants, were killed and also many died from starvation or infectious diseases. The imperial government, possibly any government in any other countries, responded with harsh measures against the civil disorders. The mandarins, high ranking government officials, who, most likely, had access to some food because of their wealth and influence, were not so much worried about the suffering of the people but felt the challenge to the government authority which they upheld in official capacity. The harshness of the official response reflected the measure of the threat the governing body felt, that is, the instinct of self-preservation. Possibly this is the general policy that applies even today to the government as well as to the individuals: if these bodies are criticised or attacked they meet with all the forces available for them.

The government officials beheaded the rioters or put the law breakers into 'sorrow cage' where they were left till they died. If the famine was of benign nature, the mandarins could handle the disturbances and the good harvests in a few years' time quieted the population. However, if the famine spread to the large area of China and of a serious nature, the government could not cope with the situation. Total chaos could easily degenerate to large scale battles between the government forces and the rebel army. A capable rebel leader came up and became the head of the rebel army which challenged the authority of the reigning emperor. If the challenging army had strong support of people and the government army was disorganised, the rebel leader defeated the regular army decisively and killed or deposed the emperor. The new leader became an emperor people and Heaven sanctioned.

As a matter of fact, people did not have any other choice but to approve the newly appointed emperor in the absence of the strong oppositions. In the first place, he became victorious in the conflicts because people supported him and could repel any further challenge, if any arose. In the second place he was the only hope to restore order, a good government and food. By this time a huge number of people were dead and scarce food, stored or harvested, may be just enough to go around the remaining population. If that was not the case, more people had to die from starvation and infectious diseases, if not from war acts. In due course good harvests arrived to relieve people of the suffering, and the new emperor and government were stabilised. The new dynasty went on until the next cycle of overpopulation forced another dynastic change in the similar fashion.

The corruption of the ruling class and shortage of food because of adverse weather seem to be two different matters to us. However, for the hungry people, the logic was not important and they insisted on change of the ruling dynasty.

At the time of dynastic changeover, the following requirements were intricately interwoven:

- The population had to reduce to a point where the remaining people can find some food--from the stored grains or new harvests.
- The victorious rebel leader had to be seen morally on high ground and consequently being capable both militarily and politically.

Only when the above two conditions were met, people regarded the new leader sanctioned by Heaven and looked up at him as a new emperor.

The foregoing explanation of dynastic change is obviously over simplified. A good emperor possibly averted the acute food shortage by efficient administration. His bureaucracy would have organised to store grains during good harvests. It would have engineered transportation of crops to the provinces where the serious harvest failures occurred. It is on record that some emperors carried out these measures systematically but they counted little under the severe food shortage. It is reasonably expected that under good administration the hungry peasants would not have directed their anger to the respected emperor but to some convenient targets. When a bad emperor had ruled during serious shortage of food, the problems would have been exasperated, and the termination of the dynasty would have eventuated. The above terms, describing the emperors as good, bad or respected, are certainly not precise but I am sure that the Chinese people felt one way or another depending on the perceived characters of the reigning emperors. People thought that the righteous emperor would institute good policies in the same way people have thought beautiful women would have good minds. Both assumptions are not necessarily correct. In the first place people's perception can be wrong. Even the righteous emperor may not have an ability to place good policies and also he may make a mistake. Ethical people, if trained properly, can handle most jobs in the society but only the select few can handle the emperor's job with competency.

Some modern scholars attributed the cause of dynastic change to overpopulation. It is also a speculation in modern times that Shih huang-ti initiated the vast construction works whose ulterior motive was to eliminate surplus population. Even some seers had known the problem of overpopulation in relation to the limited land, and preached reduced population in an official or private capacity, it would have landed on deaf ears. The heated dogs and cats cannot be effectively restrained from sex by telling them of unwanted consequence of too many offspring. In a similar way, men cannot be told effectively to refrain from sex by telling them of bad consequences of overpopulation, adultery and spread of diseases. The males of these species just cannot stop having sex. China was not ready to embrace such a measure of birth control until sometime after the establishment of the People's Republic of China in 1949. Even Malthus did not preach a reduced number of people. Though he set up the proposition that the overpopulation was the fundamental cause of war, starvation, poverty and general misery, he took the view that no body, government or individual, should interfere with the process. He thought it natural that people paid the consequence of their stupidity. (Spielvogel 1991, p. 746)

Modern China

It was claimed that the modern China began in 1919, when Chen Duxiu cried aloud, 'Destroy the old curiosity shop of Confucius!'

It seems that China, which the Manchu (Ch'ing) dynasty governed since 1644, was approaching the end of the dynastic cycle in the early part of the 20th century. The Manchus, being ethnically different from the Chinese, are members of Mongoloid people of Manchuria and conquered China in 1644. The Manchu was known as the Jurchen from the late T'ang to the Ming dynasties. (Lopez 1996, p. 223)

China knew no peace and passed through the phases of disintegration from 1840s to 1949. The problem became acute particularly in the early 20th century and millions of Chinese people died from starvation, internal wars and foreign invasions. The years 1911-49 are often called the period of disunion in China.

The shih (the gentry and scholars) lost the avenue of the advancement and influence in the state organisation in the wake of the abolition of the state examination system in 1905, and the fall of the last Confucian dynasty in 1911/1912. The opening of modern schools caused a massive inflow of Western ideas among the nung (the peasant farmers). The Confucian classics lost their influence which had been virtually undisputed since the Han Empire. (Cotterell & Morgan 1975, p. 265)

In connection with the rise of rebellions in China in the 19th century, the gentry (scholar-officials) played an important role. When the rebellions were widespread, the central government had to rely on the gentry class for support. One thing the government did was to increase the number of the gentry. The gentry group consisted of:

- those who had obtained admission by passing the examinations,
- those who had obtained titles or offices by purchase, thus giving the government a large amount of revenue.

In the first half of the 19th century the gentry class amounted to 1.1 million, and subsequently more gentry was created totalling 1.45 million for both categories of the gentry group.

Another measure the government allowed was that the gentry collected taxes and formed the militia to combat the rebellions (Roberts 1998, p. 59).

In the properly maintained Confucian state harmony prevailed. The various calamities that overtook China were attributed to the failure to maintain Confucian ideology. Hence the remedy for the misfortune had to be to install upright Confucian officials. (p. 65)

Feng Guifen (Feng Kuei-fen), Chinese scholar, recognised the superiority of Western science and technology. Accordingly Zhang Zhidong, Ch'ing official, promulgated the policy known as self-strengthening in 1860, though it did not become at this time the national policy the national government endorsed. One thrust of the strengthening was to put forward Western technology and armament industries in China. However, in the Sino-Japanese War (1894-5) China suffered humiliating defeat on land and sea, and the self-strengthening of the previous decades was assessed as unsuccessful. (p. 68-9)

Cixi (Tz'u-hsi), Empress Dowager, the dominant force at court throughout this period, did not fully cooperate with the policy of the self-strengthening if not obstructive. The government role was crucial in promoting the industries for the countries such as China which were late comers to the modern technology. (p. 76)

The Chinese bureaucracy was geared to strengthen the agrarian economy and did not have the expertise to develop the industries. The government also lacked the capital for the development of unfamiliar industries. Particularly the armament industries did not produce any profits. (p. 77)

Modern China had to bear the economic effects of Western imperialism. China in the eighteenth century was a prosperous agrarian country. By the middle of the 20th century she appeared to be poor and underdeveloped. (p. 91)

Taiping Rebellion (1850-64)

Starting towards the end of the 18th century, China suffered a series of rebellions which came close to overthrowing the Ch'ing dynasty. Two major rebellions were:

- White Lotus Rebellion (1796-1804)
- Taiping Rebellion (1850-64)

(Roberts 1998, p. 43)

The rises of rebellions in China were traditionally interpreted as the decline of dynasty. Confucian historians looked at history in terms of dynastic cycles. The most detrimental factor to destabilise was the population growth. In the late 17th century China's population was about 150 million. A hundred years later the population doubled. One way of solving the overpopulation was for the Han Chinese to migrate into the depopulated area away from the densely populated coastal regions. For example, the Manchu government sponsored the migration of the Chinese to such area as Sichuan. Also the present Chinese government encourage the Chinese migration into Tibet. The migration of this nature not only removes the population pressure from the densely populated area but at the same time proceeds with sinification of the remote regions in terms of people, culture and politics. (p. 44)

The deaths resulting from the rebellions offered some relief from the population pressure (p. 59).

The White Lotus society was the Buddhist sect established in the 13th century and engineered the overthrow of the foreign rules, the Yuan and Manchu.

The Taiping Rebellion, the greatest uprising in the world history, led to huge destruction and to the loss of between 20 and 30 million lives. This rebellion was unusual in that it looked outside Chinese civilisation for inspiration, that is, Christianity. The Taipings were a semi-religious group that combined Christian belief with ancient Chinese ideas for perfect society. The Taiping Rebellion began in July 1850 and the rebels captured Nanjing in March 1853.

The Red Turban Revolt (1854-7) began in July 1854. The Red Turban Rebellion resulted from the rival clans' hostility between the Hakka and the Punti in Guangdong, which came to the open battles during the unrest in the neighbouring areas. The conflicts resulted in over one million deaths and contributed to the disintegration of the reigning government.

The Taipings challenged the Qing (Ch'ing) dynasty, denouncing Confucianism and proposing to divide the land equally among the people. It failed miserably. (Cotterell & Morgan 1975, p. 240) The gentry-led regional armies contained the rising in the end. The scholar-officials, alarmed by anti-Confucian stance of the rebels, sided with the Ch'ing dynasty. The Ch'ing dynasty's success in suppressing this rebellion can be taken as evidence that the Chinese gentry fully sided with it. Uprisings on the scale of the Taiping Rebellion had toppled many dynasties: the Yellow Turbans brought down the Han; White Lotus rebels destroyed the Yuan; and Li Zicheng (Li Tzu-ch'eng) brought an end to the Ming. The failure of the Taiping Rebellion gave new ammunition to oppose Christianity. (Ebrey 1996, pp. 100, 243)

<u>Great Famine of 1876-9</u>

The drought induced famine gripped northern China for three years beginning in the autumn of 1876 and this is said to be the most severe famine in modern times (Ward 1989, pp. 132-3). Drought is the most common natural cause of famine. It is estimated that totally 13 million people eventually died from starvation, diseases and the subsequent civil disorders. Cannibalism became rife. The farmers sold their daughters into prostitution and their sons into slavery and a large number of people became bandits.

If the theory that the fundamental cause of the dynastic change is shortage of agricultural land in the face of the overpopulation, in short, lack of food, as in this case, holds right, why did this famine not bring the fall of the Ch'ing dynasty (1644-1911 or 1912) then reigning? Or the above theory wrong? Certainly the lack of land did not cause this famine but adverse weather induced, which would have had the same effect to the general public anyway. Let me answer the question in the following way.

The Ch'ing dynasty was in a healthy state at that time though going through the period of disintegration in a broad assessment, and did not act in a way to deserve the end of the ruling family, though it is true that this dynasty was weak and undistinguished except for the two capable emperors at the beginning. The positive thinking was clearly shown in the fact that the Chinese government did a great deal to try to alleviate the problem rather than to meet the civil disorders with the violent measures as was traditionally the case. The right attitude of the mandarins was also reflected in the coordination of the international relief efforts for the first time in the Chinese history. (p. 135)

Apart from the above government initiatives, there were a couple of other reasons why the total collapse of the social order within China did not occur in spite of the severity of the famine under discussion.

The Great Famine referred to did not spread to the entire China but was confined to the provinces in the northern China. Thus the surplus food of the other provinces was transported to the affected regions. Without bringing in the food from the outside, more people would have died. The surviving people would have been grateful for the government assistance. There was another peculiar aspect to the whole episode concerning the people's characters of the northern China. People in these regions were used to disasters. In the past 3000 years, the Yellow River has flooded the Northern China Plain some 1500 times, though never with more destructiveness as in late September 1887 (pp. 136-7) which occurred several years after the end of the Great Famine. Thus these people were accustomed to starvation from drought or flood and were conditioned to put up with any hardship. As a consequence many people died in silence and the surviving people did not try to wreck the government.

There is one important lesson we can draw from this Great Famine. The food shortage itself, however serious it may be, cannot be the only cause of the dynastic fall and there must be other reasons existing at the same time to bring about the collapse of the reigning imperial family. Also the food shortage because of adverse weather in a local area is different from the land shortage which covers the entire China and gives rise to food shortage on the permanent basis to a large part of China.

In the last decade of the nineteenth century and the first three decades of the twentieth, Western philosophy was popular in China. During the first decade of the twentieth century, the Ch'ing dynasty was undermined simultaneously on nearly every front. In modern China, Western democratic ideals and the Marxist doctrine after 1917 were overlaid over the traditional Chinese culture and the imperial claims. There was also an anti-Confucian campaign in China during the early 1970s under the communist rule. (Koller 1985, pp. 331, 338)

Simmering tension between foreign interests in China and fanatical anti-Western Chinese patriots broke out into savage bloodshed, called the Boxer Rebellion (1899-1901). The rebellion erupted spontaneously across north China with no unifying leader. The members combined popular religious practices with martial arts. The slogan was 'Support the Qing (Ch'ing) and destroy the foreign'. (Harris 1999, p. 72) Cixi (Tz'u-hsi), Empress Dowager, sided with the rebels. The defeat of the rebels brought a ghastly revenge by the Westerners to the people of Peking, and a humiliating treaty of 1901. This defeat of the boxers and earlier by the hand of the Japanese brought the eventual downfall of the Ch'ing dynasty in 1912. (Davison 1993, pp. 282-3)

The Ch'ing court itself was edging to the direction of constitutionalism and parliamentary government. In 1905 the civil service examinations were abolished and the steps were taken to set up both a modern school system and a modern government bureaucracy. (Ebrey 1996, p. 264) In 1908 the Dowager Tz'u-hsi died of natural causes at the age of 73 and the strength of the Ch'ing dynasty was spent. The conditions of the country and the misery of its people indicated that the Ch'ing dynasty had lost its Heavenly Mandate. (Grenville 1994, p. 79)

From 1905 to 1911, the rebels staged a series of unsuccessful military attacks against the government. In 1911 the revolution to overthrow the Manchus started. (p. 81) On October 10, 1911, the army troops revolted at Wuchang. By the year's end the southern and central provinces declared their independence from the Manchu rule.

The Manchu (Ch'ing) dynasty survived Tz'u-hsi by only three years, until 1911, when the monarchy was overthrown and the republic established by the revolutionary reformers led by Sun Yat-sen. He is often called Father of the Revolution; however, his thoughts were too idealistic to be an effective political leader. China at the time was under so massive a foreign debt that it was virtually in subjugation to the Western powers. (Davison 1993, p. 285)

In December 1911, the leaders of revolution met to establish a republic and named Sun Yixian (Sun Yat-sen) temporary president of the republic. In February 1912, the last Ch'ing emperor, a 6 year old boy named Puyi (P'u-i), abdicated, and in March Sun Yat-sen, back in China, issued a provisional constitution. (Ebrey 1996, p. 166) After a secret settlement, on March 10, 1912, Yuan Shikai (Yuan Shih-k'ai), a retired military official, became president in place of Sun Yat-sen. Yuan Shikai expanded his power and tried to become an emperor himself. The strong opposition forced him to abandon the idea of establishing an empire and he died in 1916.

> Most peasants had seen no improvement in their standard of living since Qing (Ch'ing) times. Continued population growth--by 1930 the figure was over 500 million--resulted in relentless increase in the pressure on available land. (p. 278)

Political and intellectual revolutionaries of the early twentieth century China all spoke out in the need to change ways of thinking about women and their social roles (p. 279). They preached both to abandon foot binding and to encourage education of women.

Section 3, Chapter 1, Book Three *Communism* describes briefly how communism triumphed in China.

The communist leader by the name of Mao Zedong emerged as a victor and established a new dynasty in 1949. Though the revolution was carried out for the sake of the communist ideology, the pattern of dynastic change due to food scarcity was evident in the process.

In both Russia and China, the communists became dominant in the chaotic period when the central authority had ceased to operate for some time. The industrial workers were the core activists of the Russian Revolution. Though the hammer, the symbol of industry, and the sickle, the symbol of farming, were given an equal place in the national flag of the USSR, the industries were given the first priority for development. In fact the farming sector, though collectivised during the Stalin's reign, did not develop as much as it should have through the communist rule. It was shown in such subsequent events as five to seven million people died as the result of the famines in 1932 and 1933, and also the USSR had to import the grains in the 1970s. The collectivisation was in a sense industrialisation of farming, resulting from the industrial workers' desire to impose their way of life on the farmers. In contrast, in China, the peasants were the backbone of the Communist Revolution; however, there is no evidence that its policies favoured farming rather than the industry. Ironically the overall success in the production of the farm products led to the huge increase of its population, which became the fundamental problem of the Chinese communist party.

The Chinese Communist Party as a whole did not realise for many years after the revolution that China's population explosion would have most detrimental effect on the economic future of the country, wiping out all the gains the revolution achieved. It seems that the party officials were busy formulating communistic policies and did not take to heart the concept of the dynastic cycles of history as their problem. Mao himself was not aware of the problem all his life, which is said to be his greatest mistake. The party became conscious of the seriousness of the unrestricted population growth after Mao's death in1976, and went ahead with formulating and implementing drastic family planning of one child policy. This policy was imposed in China in 1981; however, the ethnic minority (5% of the total population) was exempted. According to this policy, one married couple can have only one child and no more. The scheme is drastic to the extreme because according to the statistical study a mother can have, with today's medical standard, on average 2.1 children to ensure static population, compensating for the various wastages, natural and man-made. (Spielvogel 1991, p. 1034)

> The Chinese government does not interfere into everyday affairs to the extent it used to. However, it still has a tremendous coercive force, as witnessed to force adherence to a very unpopular birth limitation programme and to silence most of its critics. (Ebrey 1996, p. 331)

One child policy has widespread resentment among the mass of the Chinese people. It is widely rumoured that many newly-born girls are killed in secret in the hope to have a baby boy in the future, for the Chinese family traditionally favours a boy. Undeterred by wide-spread infanticide, the government seems determined to carry on with the strict restriction order. That is understandable since, as the party sees, the overpopulation can not only annul the achievement of their proud revolution but may bring about another dynastic change whose course is hard even to theorise. In spite of the enthusiasm of the party officials on this policy, I heard from a woman who visited China recently--around 1990--that one child policy was effectively enforced in cities but was ignored in many rural areas.

The next passage is one assessment of the one child policy of government initiative:

> The population of China about doubled between 1949 and 1990, despite the imposition of one child policy in 1981 and despite the worst famine in the world history from 1958 to 1963 when over 30 million Chinese starved to death. The imposition of one child policy is not effective in the country side where nearly 80 percent of Chinese still live. (Murowchick 1994, p. 31)

The deaths of 30 million Chinese as the result of the above famine, though some said it was government policy failure, hardly dented the Chinese population which grew from 500 million in 1949 to 1 billion in 1990. The fact of the matter was that in spite of the above famine the communist rule did not collapse.

The most recent report (2009) from China says that the Chinese people reversed the preference on children and prefer to have daughters instead of sons as was the tradition. Pendulum swang to the other way after moving to one direction too far, and the latest survey indicates that the Chinese families wanting daughters outnumber those wanting boys. There were many reasons for the change. Too many boys—120 boys for 100 girls—caused social problems such as prostitution and sex crimes. People challenged the traditional views. People realised that it was more expensive to raise boys than girls. Girls tend to care for the aged. People changed the practice of dowries and buying houses. Also the government enacted the social security to minimise the various problems.

Overall Assessment of Concept of Chinese Dynastic Cycles

After the introduction of farming in a region its population seemed to be ever on the increase until something tangible, for example, war, disease or simply lack of food, prevented this growing trend. Thus it is not an exaggeration to say that a country was inhabited by the largest number of people supportable with the knowledge and various resources available at the time. The bulk of the population kept having children, seemingly not caring about the consequences of both the oversizing of the family and the overpopulation of the country.

We could look at even the industrialisation as an attempt to enlarge the supportable population. Improvement in medical knowledge and public health dramatically curtailed the death rates without decline of the birth rates. The newly set-up industries employed a large number of people who could afford to buy food and support their families. New techniques and machines made possible more efficient agriculture. Imports in exchange for the industrial goods met the shortage of food, if any at all. Thus the industrialisation enabled to support more mouths with the same land area.

There have been two major population explosions in the course of human social evolution. The introduction of agriculture in the Neolithic age was one. The introduction of machine manufacture, the so-called Industrial Revolution, was another. It was in Western Europe, with the Industrial Revolution which started in Britain in 1760, that the second population explosion began. Europe's population doubled during the 18th century, from roughly 100 million to nearly 200 million, and doubled again during the 19th century, to about 400 million.

We can see the trend in Japan clearly. Japan had the population of 33 million in 1868 when it was a feudal society and the Meiji Restoration was announced. In 1897 when the industrialisation was beginning to accelerate, it had the population of 42 million. In 1920, 57 million. By 1940 the population of Japan was 70 million, which was more than double that of 1868. After World War II, the industrialisation of Japan continued going beyond the restoration of the plants destroyed by the war and its population kept growing. Its population reached 100 million in 1960, the triple of that of 1968. It reached 126 million in 1996.

However, the trend of ever increasing population with industrialisation seemed to have stopped in many economically advanced countries through education in recent times. Well-educated people generally learned the futility of having a large family. Most of them now practise the family planning to have a small number of children, thinking that a small family is better for themselves, for the children and for the country.

It stands to reason, as the concept of dynastic cycles tells, that the food shortage gave rise to civil disturbances and at the limit caused dynastic change in China, through its history. We can also give credence to the notion that the rise and fall of an individual and a dynasty originate in the approval and disapproval by Heaven of Chinese source and God of Jewish source. Further Heaven and God make judgements according to certain criteria which primarily depend on the faith of the bodies involved.

Of course, as for any other theories proposed to explain the historical phenomena, some critics reject the notion that the population explosion is the fundamental cause of the Chinese dynastic cycles. Even if we concur to the overpopulation as the underlying cause of the dynastic change, we have to acknowledge that other causes, in addition, must have been present for the dynastic change to perpetuate. The bad influence of eunuchs, the weakened court, and the siding of the gentry class against the ruling dynasty were also cited as the contributing causes of some of the dynastic changeovers. The overpopulation and the economic downturn may be the two sets of unrelated phenomena, and we may have to separate the two for our analyses. However, it is generally agreed that the overpopulation was the main cause of the dynastic cycles in China.

China as we know as an empire has a history of approximately 2200 years and it has been unified perhaps half of that duration under the effective central government. The ruling houses of parts or even all of China came from alien origin for some 700 years. (Loewe 1990, p. 49) We can see that the native empire as dreamed by many Chinese scholars was hardly the norm during the history of 2200 years. Hence the critics of the foregoing theory argue that one of the fundamental causes of dynastic cycles was in fact the conquest of China by detested foreigners, though some of subjugation may have coincided with the low ebb of the dynasty as well as with the shortage of food. However, contrary to the above general statement, the Sung dynasty was vigorous; the Jurchens and then the Mongols were too powerful militarily and the Sung court eventually succumbed. In the face of the overwhelming superiority of the Mongol army, the arguments that the Sung economy was in good or bad shape or the Sung court was corrupt or not were in fact irrelevant. Conquest by foreigners led to the setting up of a new dynasty and the restoration of Chinese rule led to the setting up of a native dynasty.

Jurchen and Mongol conquests of China were detrimental not only to the economy but to the healthy population growth. The Jurchens occupied all of northern China in 1127 and formed the Chin dynasty. However, the Jurchen empire was destroyed in 1234 as the result of the alliance between the Mongols in the north and the Sung in the south. Kublai Khan founded the Yuan dynasty in China in 1279 and 'in 1290 the registered population of China was down to 60 million, and was still at that level a century later'. (Ebrey 1996, p. 184) The Manchus in Manchuria were descended from the Jurchens who also lived in Manchuria.

According to the traditional Chinese history, the three dynasties of Han, T'ang and Ming fell because of the evil influence of the eunuchs on the government. It is hard for us to believe the eunuchs alone had such a power as to bring down the ruling house unless the emperor and the government bureaucracy were corrupt and consequently disapproved by Heaven. It is said that T'ang and Ming were economically in good shape when they were terminated.

We also have to look at the philosophical aspect of the dynasty's rise and fall. We must examine the growth and decline of the individual human beings as well as of the society, assuming that there is a good correlation between the two. In general for an individual and for a nation, people feel happy at prosperity but make little progress as human beings and the seeds of troubled times to come are sown at this time. People feel miserable at adversity but make good progress, unknowingly to themselves, as human beings and the seeds of good times to come are sown at this time. People's experience and learning tell them that their characters and way of thinking improve a great deal under hardships. It is beyond dispute that the hardships make better people or better nations, provided the people do not go astray, by corrupting themselves. Many good people testify that they became mature only through suffering.

In fact, all the major thoughts of life in China came into being during the Warring States period (481 or 403-221 BC). Especially the two major ideologies, Confucianism and Daoism, born during this troubled times together with Buddhism which came forth in India during its troubled times, made crucial contributions to the Chinese way of life through the centuries until the Communist Revolution. In this light, the concept of dynastic cycles, whatever causes we may ascribe to them, seems pretty useless: Chinese people discovered new thoughts and matured through adversity rather than the good times unified by emperors.

Section 3 Exploitation

The Bible makes frequent allusions to the oppressions and exploitations not only in interpersonal relationships within a society but also interracial relationships in an international arena. It regards the instances of oppression as evils though it does not regard these evils inherent in the social system. There is no mention of attacking the social institutions such as slavery, family, social organisation, ruler-ruled relationship and social hierarchy. The authors of the Testaments address the people not to oppress the widows, the orphans and the aliens because God will avenge for their sake. Specifically the Testaments urge the people in authority not to exploit the people under their care because God sees it as evil. They advise the weak and vulnerable people such as mentioned above not to despair of the oppression because God will help them in the end if they have faith in God. The Bible tries to solve the problem of exploitation through faith in God.

The central theme of Marxism was the abolition of the social exploitation. Karl Marx got to know the dreadful state of the working people in England during and just after the Industrial Revolution (1760-1840). He preached that only the new social system could solve the problem of exploitation in conjunction with the employment. He wrote that only the establishment of a new society based on his doctrine of communism could eliminate the exploitation within the society. Communism was, in a sense, a social system which was designed to create a society with no systematic exploitation. If the capitalist system can eliminate the social exploitation, I would say that there is no need to introduce communism. For the research into communism and Karl Marx see Chapter 1 Communism Appraised, Book Three *Communism*.

As I understand, one of the fundamental theories Marx put forward is that of surplus value, in an attempt to explain and even to eliminate exploitation. In a production environment, the wage labourers offer their services for a set amount of money. The capitalists receive revenues by selling the products thus manufactured: the incoming money should be greater than the outgoing money which pays for raw materials, wages and depreciation of the equipment. The difference between the total revenue and total expenditure, that is, the profit at this stage, is called surplus value. Marx sometimes assumed surplus value to be the same amount as the aggregate of all wages, though he did not even try to prove the premise. Another strange proposition he made was that all rents associated with production, whether it be for building or land, must be paid by this surplus value. 'Rent is a surplus, not a cost of production.' (Heimann 1964, p. 196) Some capitalist economists, for instance, Marshall, also supported the view (Robbins 1998, p. 190). To my way of thinking, rents are a part of production aids, hence should be classed as the expenditure in the same way as the production cost, that is, the rent should not be included in profit in the first place.

Marx argued that only the wage labourers contributed to the creation of surplus value. He did not recognise that the capitalists and even the managers have any claims to the surplus money, in spite of the fact that the capitalists provide all means of production and the managers make all important decisions in running the factory. He concluded that the capitalists and managers do not contribute to the production process, and the wage labourers can take over the role of the managers without any dislocation of production when the state takes over all the production facilities from the capitalists under the communist rule. There is no illogicality that the state, not the capitalists, will own all the production facilities under the communist rule. He wrote repeatedly in his works that as a consequence of the above logic all the surplus value rightfully belongs to the wage labourers but the capitalist system permits the capitalists to get hold of it. This is the system of exploitation under capitalism he so decried of. This reasoning of exploitation is cited to justify the proletarian revolution: the proletariats (wage labourers) have every right to forcefully acquire all the production means without compensation to the capitalists. However, there is definitely an illogicality in the proposition that the wage labourers takes over the function of the managers, that is, the wage labourers become managers individually or even as a group.

Let's turn our attention to Karl Marx's family life since this may give some clues to the bases of his claims. He did not make any economic assessment of family life, and his main interest was directed to the economic activities of firms and nations, though he accused 'the bourgeoisie has torn the veil of sentimentality away from the family and has reduced the family relation to a mere money relation' (Marx & Engels 1989, p. 115).

It is generally thought that the family is a place of affection and the firm a place of disaffection. I have found through my experience that this assessment is not necessarily true. Both can be a source of sorrow and joy and both can be a source of exploitation. Some people are emotionally attached to their family or firm. Some people change the family as easily as some do with the firm. In these lights there is a good deal common to the two human establishments. Karl Marx must have thought that the firms produced something tangible such as goods and lesser degree services and that the families were outside the range of social considerations. However, there is no question that the family organisations are quite important human establishment which is supposed to give security and comforts to the members as well as to produce children. Frederick Engels wrote that the determining factor in history according to the materialistic conception is the production of necessities of life as well as the propagation of people (Marx & Engels 1970, p. 191).

Karl Marx married a childhood sweetheart, a beautiful woman of aristocratic origin and had three daughters by her. She bore four more babies but they did not survive. Marx also had a child by the maidservant who lived with the Marx family. Before the 20th century, women in Europe did not have the right to vote and normally did not hold professional jobs. Consequently they had to be supported by somebody else, most likely by their parents before marriage and by their husbands after marriage unless they own considerable assets or hold jobs with insultingly low wages. It seems that Marx's wife did not get substantial financial help from her family and the family expense had to be met by Marx, Friedrich Engels, and at later years pensions.

One of the thrusting theories of Marxism lay in the presumption that economic motivation ultimately decided the human activities, though he emphasised the thrust of the group rather than the decisions of the individual. The fact that Marx married and had so many children went directly against the above assumption. If he had stayed single, he would have had only himself to support. However, by marrying he ended up supporting two females and a number of children until the children were to grow up and leave the family home. In point of fact his wife died in 1881 and the eldest daughter died two years later. Marx did not recover from these misfortunes and died in 1883. The two of his remaining daughters committed suicide; one in 1898 and the other in 1911. He occasionally theorised that his income, if he works for a firm, would be only half of his contribution to his employer, and the capitalist would exploit off the rest. Yet he had to feed several extra mouths in his family apart from himself, thus his share of the income was drastically curtailed--much less than half.

Though the above line of reasoning does not take into account tax advantage, the probability that his children will support him in his old age and the personal satisfaction derived from rearing a family. Also, his wife contributed to him sexually, domestically and as a companion. If he had obtained sex, domestic service and a companion on the market, the total fees would have amounted to a large sum, especially for a large family such as his. The comparison I am seeking in this section is between singleness and the family life, and not the family life and the professional service. I am sure that purely on the financial transactions, he would have been better off if he had stayed single and saved money for his old age.

I have come to believe that the reason why Marx did not see the above obvious fault is that he did not practise the conformity of speech and conduct. This correspondence was one major fruit of the idealist pursuits culminated at the early classical era in a few parts of the world, as I propound in D Conformance of Speech and Conduct, Section 3, Chapter 7, Book One. Both Socrates and Confucius in particular strongly advocated what they instructed must be the reflection of how they lived: Anybody who dares to teach other people in ethics must base their teachings on his daily life. Marx's theories, though in politico-economic discipline, contain not only what it is but in the large measure what ought to be and can be classed to be normative, prophetic or moral, hence the foregoing requirement applies. Marx did not lead his life as he taught and consequently he did not see such an obvious and striking gap between his teaching and his personal life. It is interesting to note that the teaching of conformity is not mere rhetoric but has a practical use as I point out here.

Karl Marx wrote that marriage was an institution under which men subjugated and exploited women and children. It was generally true in Europe before the 20th century that men dominated within the family and regarded their wives and children as their property. However, in this day and age this notion is no longer acceptable in the civilised societies and each member of the family has a justifiable claim to a partnership, equal for women and partial for children before adulthood, in the family enterprise.

Marx's chief fault on this matter lay, I believe, in his assumption that male dominance in the family was inherent in the capitalist society. He made a similar erroneous assumption when he stated that the employers exploited the employees in the productive environment. Certainly what he stated about the family and corporation was extensively observed in the European societies of Marx's life time. These phenomena came about only after the sustained and often vicious struggles among the contestants. Hence we can note of the opposite observations where the wives and the workers dominated the scene in the isolated instances of the early 20th century Europe, and this trend, in both domestic and industrial environment, is becoming increasingly common in the latter part of the 20th century. For example, in today’s work environment, the workers have sick and various compensation entitlements and the union determinations.

Men dominated their family not only by their higher levels of physical and mental capabilities but through clever manipulation of their earnings. The social custom did not make automatically the bread winners leaders of the family. Whenever the wives had advantageous resources available for them, they dominated the family. If the wives bring a large wealth at the time of marriage, they naturally try to take an advantageous position with their husbands. However, in the general conflicts between the two parties outside marriage, wealth is sometimes a boon and sometimes a bane.

The similar reasoning applies about the relationship of the employees to the employers. The bottom line is that the employees need the jobs for money and personal satisfaction as much as the employers need people for carrying out the jobs to make money. If stated in reverse, Marx paid attention to the workers’ fear of losing their jobs but ignored the firms’ fear of losing the personnel to carry on the organisations. The latter fact is clearly shown today by the huge sum of money spent advertising the vacancies and also by the unwillingness of dismissing the employees for laziness and misconduct. Unlike the employees of Marx’s lifetime the employees of today have a fair deal of freedom of conducts, the degree of which also depending on the ranking within the organisation, before they are dismissed. Also the willingness and unwillingness to work by the employees in conjunction with exploitation often decide if the firm can go on or not in the long run. Though the employers have the powers of dismissing the workers in most occasions and of closing the factory, there are more considerations at work in the manufacturing and trading environments where these capitalists or managers bet they can make the most money under the current settings. Before they dismiss the workers they have to have the assurance that the newly employed workers are better than the workers to be dismissed, if they can get any. During the Industrial Revolution in Britain the employers were assured that they could get enough workers; in fact this is one main reason why they treated the employees harshly. Before they close the factory they have to know where they can get the better returns for their capital, apart from the loss of money at the changeover.

I am going to cite a few observations testifying that men do not automatically become leaders within the family but have to wrest the leadership by various means at whatever point of human development:

- If a young and pretty woman marries an old man whether he may be rich or poor, it is a good bet that she enslaves him.
- If the woman of substance in honour or in property gets betrothed to an insignificant man, she will most likely take a leading role in running the family, though she may be physically and mentally weaker than her husband.
- If a wife's income or prospect for promotion exceeds that of her husband, which is not rare nowadays, the wife naturally thinks she should have more say in the decision makings within the family. If the husband does not recognise this, she will fight it out until she gets her way.

The family members can be friends if they have similar characters and life views but they can be enemies if they disagree on too many issues of concern.

Who would be the boss in the family may be settled only after the husband and wife exhaust all the resources to the utmost for the better results in the same way two warring firms or nations exhaust all their resources for the better results of the conflict. The couple may or may not reach unanimous conclusion after many years of bloody fightings. Or the husband and wife may not contest at all because the outcome was obvious for both of them at the time of marriage: they had the unanimous opinion about their relative worth from the beginning.

The similar reasoning applies to the question of leadership within the firms or even among the nations, though in the case of the firms, the higher authority or the owners decide the leadership issue rather than the competing individuals in the family and the competing nations among the nations. The families, firms and nations are all human organisations. Though their characteristics are different in some way, they show similar traits in many respects such as the leadership question.

Another point Marx did not see was that the wives and children in fact financially exploit their husbands within the family if only the husbands work. The husbands have to spend money to give their spouses and kids food, clothes, shelter, and some form of amusements apart from children’s education. Here again it is the subjective feeling that makes the distinction between exploitation and non-exploitation. Parenting is exploitation if the parents think so; it is not exploitation if the parents think not. Many people may object to the use of the term exploitation in this context, saying that men get into matrimony voluntarily and it is not logical to say men wanted to be exploited and also the bonding of the family members is affection, not money. However, even in the case of employment men get into contract voluntarily. If the affection disappears from the family and only the institution remains, the bread winners may justifiably feel that they are cheated out of their incomes. If the whole family is happy, nobody feels cheated but still the monetary flow is there.

I believe that the surprising fact of life is that the monetary drain from the husbands is a form of exploitation in the family: in Marx's era it was a norm since only men under the normal circumstances had the well-paid jobs outside the family. This reality imposes varying degrees of strain and consequently some resentment on men, though responsible men may be reluctant to express it openly since they are the ones who took the lead in initiating the family. Besides, many of them feel that they have no choice but to carry the burden until their children can support themselves. Still we often hear about monetary and managing problems within the family and also about the husbands who cannot bear the pressures and run away. The chief difficulty in the use of the word 'exploitation' here is that we cannot assess emotional aspects concerning socialisation and affection within the family in terms of money.

Karl Marx focused his attention to the dominance within the family and wrote that the husbands exploited their wives and children. If we paid attention to the monetary flow of the family unit, the wives and children exploited the husbands. Whichever way people looked at the family, the onus was on the adult males to look after the rest of the family members, though this concept has been seriously challenged in recent years. Thus the average males were exploited by their employers and were again exploited financially by their dependants in the family. When people looked at the magnitude of the monetary drain, I am sure that the exploitation in the family was more pronounced than that in employment for the majority of men. This was definitely the case with Marx since he had few regular incomes with so many dependants until he got the government pension. Surprisingly Marx did not see this reality, which makes a mockery of his voluminous papers on surplus value and his spiteful attack on the employer exploitation. If my view is correct, the entire ideology of communism reduces to lots smaller dimensions. Thomas Hobbes put the matter in *Leviathan* (1651) better than Marx did in this respect. Hobbes declared the fundamental human relations as: War of every man against every other man (Hutchins 1952, pp. 85-6), which existed not only within the families, firms and nations but among these organisations. The breakdown of the absolute authority on the part of the husbands probably led to the recent tendency of the family breakdowns. For example, in the Roman Empire, the husbands had the authority to kill the rest of the family: Under this authority, it is hard for us to see that the family breaks down easily.

There is another serious deficiency in the exploitation theories Karl Marx propounded. As a rule of thumb, one-third of the working people in the industrialised nations today—I am assessing Marx's theories to the actualities of today's societies--are employed by the private companies; they include industrial workers, tenant farmers, domestic servants and shop assistants. One-third belong to the governments of various levels. One-third are self-employed or family enterprises; they include the farmers, shop owners and independent tradespeople. 'In Australia today, three-quarters of all firms are operated by their owners. But the companies account for 90% of business sales.' (McTaggart, Findley & Parkin 1992, p. 187)

Marx's theories on politico-economy are generally applicable only to the first category of employment, that is, the private firms. Throughout his theses he ignored this fact and proceeded with his argument as if he had covered all the cases of employment. Thus his theory of exploitation applies, if correct at all, only to the workers who came under the first category. The self-employed people or family enterprises do not have the exploitation issue between the employers and the employed, though they have to deal with exploitation within the family and also with other businesses.

In the public service, as I observed from my own experience working there, the working people in general exploited the government. Public servants at all levels produced little outputs yet the various statutes and conventions protected them. When a public servant got into strife by making a serious mistake or by sheer incompetence, they normally could wriggle out of it by cleverly lying. I was surprised to learn how clever and enthusiastic these people were when trying to get out of the difficulty they themselves had created, though the same people had not shown much competence and enthusiasm in their jobs. The government departments normally ran in the red, which did not surprise even the most conscientious people within or outside the government.

Before the industrialisation of the various nations of the world, the farmers (owners and tenants), and shop (of trade and manufacturing) owners and their employees made up by far the largest group of workers. The public sector in Europe expanded tremendously since Marx's contemporary societies. However, Marx's theories were developed focused on manufacturing industries of the industrialised nations.

My Experience on Exploitation

Karl Marx focused his attention on the monetary aspect of the employer-employee relationship and declared that the employers always exploited the employees. He claimed that this amounted to surplus value which was equivalent to the wages paid to the employees—though he varied the rate at times--hence the aggregate of the surplus value for a firm is equal to the aggregate of the wages the firm pays. He also claimed that the exploitation process was inherent in the social systems known up to that time as slavery, feudalism and capitalism excepting for the communal (primitive) society; and further only communism could end the unfortunate relationship.

Under the above heading we are not concerned with the truth or otherwise of the foregoing assertion but with the personal experience in the course of my working life. The above theory by Marx is hypothetical at best and I am trying to shed more light on the subject of exploitation from the broader perspectives including happiness or unhappiness, the feeling of being used or satisfied, in addition to monetary flow. I have adopted this approach on the belief that monetary payment is not, and should not be, the sole judgement of the human relations, even in the field of economic activity, because I have learned whatever we do to earn a living there is always non-economic elements, whose influences vary a great deal depending on the circumstances. The above approach also makes sense when we deal with the other human activities such as social activities, charity works and raising the family.

As I understand, the bases of any human transactions in their broadest sense may be the happiness of all the people involved: the transactions referred here include buying and selling, marriage, club activities, friendship and employment. When the transactions are complete, all the parties should feel happy in the varying degrees: we cannot avoid the circumstances where one party is happier than another. The notion that all sides should be totally satisfied, which does not happen very often in the real world, is unrealistic.

If I have a commodity I like to dispose of, then I should wait till a buyer appears who is prepared to pay the price that I feel happy with. I try to get as much money as I can and the buyer wants to pay as little as possible. When the transaction is complete, both the buyer and myself should be content; however, there is always some possibility that either party is not quite happy with the agreed price because of the limited time available for them and also the buyer with the quality of the commodity and of the limited budget. In addition the buyer may not be aware at the time of the transaction that the commodity is not suitable for the purpose or has a defect. However, the concluded transaction signifies that both sides take a bet that they cannot do better under the given circumstances, thus we can say that both are happy with the selling and buying deal.

Similarly, unless married couple is happy with each other most of the time, there is not much reason, except for their children and possibly some specific reason under some circumstances, why they should share their lives in this transaction called matrimony. When a person joins a club, he or she should feel happy about the club including the monetary flow and at the same time the other members should feel the same about this person. Friends are happy with one another almost by definition.

Labour is a form of commodity as Marx put it. When we sell our labour to the employers, both parties should be happy with the remunerations, and further we with the kind of job, and the employers with the quality of our labour. As in any other transactions, we try to get as much as possible and the employers try to give as little as possible, though in most jobs, the remunerations are set at the time of transaction by the social convention and, for example, in Australia by the award rates which the unions, the employers and the government approve. Unless both parties reach mutually satisfactory work arrangements, they cannot and should not get into the employment agreement.

If a job is on a voluntary basis, as we often see in the charitable organisations, it would be wrong to say that the workers are being exploited though they may receive negligible monetary payment. The voluntary workers get non-monetary satisfaction. The works of this nature is rather an exception to the rules of the society when we look at the volume of the voluntary jobs in comparison with the total volume of works done in the society. The economic laws of whatever persuasions do not apply in the voluntary works.

Another example where the economic theories do not apply may be the commodities the prison labour makes. Since the labour costs are negligible, the government can make quality commodities with small costs. The idea seems good; however, the manufacturers of the same commodities bitterly complain that they cannot compete with the free labour of the prisoners.

While I was a student in Adelaide, I had to earn my own living. My absolute priority was to graduate from the university and I was just too happy to work for any employer on part time or full time, depending on my availability. The notion that I might have been exploited was ridiculous and in fact did not enter into my mind at all. I was sure the employers were happy with me since I did my best to fulfil my duty.

When we employ labour around the house, be it mowing the lawn, renovating the house or repairing the household appliances, we in many occasions call in a contractor to do the job. There are various reasons why we hire the tradespeople such as we feel lazy, do not have the skill to do the job, are not equipped to do the work or are not permitted to do by law. When the contractor completes the work, both parties should feel happy at the time of payment. However, a dispute often occurs on various grounds, such as shonky workmanship or misunderstanding as to the extent of the job agreed. As a result one party or even both parties may become dissatisfied. The discontented side may feel they were exploited though we normally use ‘cheated’ or ‘tricked’ in these situations. But I cannot see any reason why we cannot use the term ‘exploitation’ in its broadest sense, since they feel they were taken advantage of, though only once.

If all the members of a family are happy, as happened in my childhood, none of them have any reason to make a gripe and to question the usefulness of the family establishment. However, if the family are engaged in constant fightings, as happened in my adolescent years, the husband may feel he is cheated out of income and the wife and children in turn may feel they are domineered unjustly by the bread winner. In this case again, it is not the flow of money but the subjective feeling of the family members which gives out the sense of exploitation. Later in my life I was convinced that the happy state of my family during my childhood was in fact false and nothing was established in the period to be entitled to be happy in the later years.

Among relatives, friends and even lovers, any occurrences of cheating and lying may be forms of exploitation.

When I was employed in the non-trade jobs, such as cleaning, processing, trade assisting or die setting, I did not feel I was exploited. Certainly there were always squabbles associated with the jobs. The unskilled works normally have a protection of a union and the remuneration is fixed often, say, throughout Australia. Besides the employers are too happy to have found people who are prepared to do the menial tasks and there is nothing much the employers can get hold of in order to exploit the unskilled workers. However, nobody can deny the possibility that the wages are less than they are entitled to and the portion of money apart from tax is already taken out of the pay packets. The fundamental fact in relation to this transaction is that the workers agree to sell their labour for the wages and the price of the labour is fixed by the agreement, though the workers may not be totally satisfied with the wages, in a similar way the seller of the commodity may not be totally satisfied with the price he is getting. The argument in this paragraph may be true in the so-called developed nations such as Australia where there are plentiful unskilled vacancies, but it is possibly not the case in underdeveloped countries with high unemployment: in the latter countries the employment for unskilled people is much harsher and more serious.

As my experience goes, the main pains in the unskilled jobs come from doing the tasks, which is inherent in these jobs in whatever social system people are in such as primitive, slavery, feudal, capitalist or communist. In this sense, changing the social system does not improve the happiness of the unskilled people in relation to the employment, since they have to go through the pains in doing the jobs under any social conditions. Certainly the better remuneration would make their life easier.

When I had professional jobs such as draftsman or engineer, I almost always got the feeling that I was exploited in some way, depending on my inexperience or weakness or desire for promotion. The employers skilfully manipulated my difficult standing to their advantage in the form of reduced salary, extra working hours without extra pay or empty promises. The above practices are widespread and many professional people will testify about it.

I am rather convinced that the employers often actively look for someone with some weaknesses whom they can use gainfully. I worked for a chief draftsman who had no technical training but was married with five children, and also for a manager who had little education but was homosexual. In both cases I thought that they were placed in the elevated positions such that their weaknesses (many children and homosexuality) can be used against them in case of trouble or dismissal, though I did not discuss the matter with any one while I worked for them. After I left the organisations, sure enough they were both removed from their jobs.

In the absence of the various difficulties, I don't think the employers can gainfully exploit the employees who are single and well experienced, even in the professional occupations. The attempt to exploit the employees does not make any distinction if they are single or not and they have weaknesses or not. However, single persons would most likely fight the injustices done on them or quit.

I graduated from the university at the age of 32 with virtually no assets. Working continuously and being single, I had enough assets at 45 to allow me to effectively retire. I now spend time doing what I like most, that is, reading and writing and also have a part-time menial job to get exercise and extra money. Even I don't get paid for my work, that is cheaper than going to the gymnasium to do exercise for the fees. Hence the idea of exploitation at work to me at this time is laughable.

In conjunction with the subject of exploitation, we must recognise the important aspects of work which the ordinary people unfortunately seem to forget or ignore. By physical and mental exertions in doing the jobs, we are training ourselves to become experts in the field of the task and also as a consequence better persons, in addition to the remunerations we receive. We are physically and mentally more capable by working hard. I have seen many people in my life who did not have the discipline to withstand the exertion and lost their jobs and the above-mentioned benefits. After so many failures they felt themselves worthless and did not want to go back to work.

In doing menial jobs, I was puzzled by one thing which was quite common occurrence in virtually all work places but manifests differently in each work place. There was always some kind of problems which did not originate in the exploitation from the management. The problems were not big because of the minor works involved; however, they can be quite irritating and upsetting to the employed persons. They were also normally of the kind which the management could remove if they seriously tried to. My query was why the managers did not eliminate the minor problems in the work place since it was their duty and within their power to do so.

One explanation was that the managers did not know the existence of the problems because the workers did not air the grievances in the atmosphere of the workplace the management generated, knowing that they would be ignored in any case. Another explanation was that the managers did not simply take up the grievances of unimportant people within the organisation. This attitude is the apathy which creates the worst kind of the work environment. Dianetics classifies the apathy of this kind to be the worst state of the mind for the individuals. Another explanation was that the managers did not comprehend the nature of the problems. Another was that because in some cases the immediate supervisor does not know the subordinate's work in details and in case of trouble, the immediate supervisor and the managers do not want to dismiss the person hence are reluctant to place the remedial instructions. Another was that the managers did not think the problems were serious enough to need their attentions. Another was that they were too lazy to do anything about the problems. Another was that they did not understand the people could be quite upsetting even the problems seemed minor to the managers if they kept occurring. Another was that the managers wanted to see the people fight under them such that they don't have a chance to attack the managers: this is the tactics of 'divide and rule' the huge empires such as Roman and British adopted.

The elimination of the problems would have made the workers happy and stay longer at the work place, increasing the productivity, all of which were for the benefits of the management as well. Also by looking into the problem at hand, the managers have the opportunity to see what is really taking place in the firm and may find a hidden problem which the employees were not aware of or even tried to hide from the management scrutiny.

The assessment that the exploitation is always subjective has an important ramification to the management. The managers can organise the firm such that the employees do not feel exploited with no extra wages and no extra work practices. I referred the good example in the foregoing paragraphs where the management was encouraged to remove the minor problems from the work places. The workers, in turn, may feel that they are fairly treated and given adequate responsibility and are prone to make minor decisions within their power and, if beyond their power, to make suggestions to the management for better running of the organisation.

Conclusions

Exploitation can happen in all spheres of human interactions, such as in the private enterprises, the government organisations, the family, and buying and selling. Possibly there are no human relationships which do not admit some forms of exploitation. I believe that discrimination is a form of exploitation. The term exploitation is used here in its broadest sense, and it is said to occur when one party takes advantage of another, unethically or unjustly, for one's own benefit, for any length of time, that is, over a long or short period or even once. Exploitation takes place, therefore, whenever one party wins over an unwary or unwilling other party through various means.

In the absence of objective measure, the only meaningful gauge to see if any exploitation is taking place must be in the subjective judgement. There is no way of ascertaining, for example, what the absolutely correct wages of the employed would be. We can get to know the social convention and the feeling of the parties involved. Because of this, some occupations command extraordinarily high wages betraying our expectations. If all the parties involved feel happy after fully knowing what was really taking place, irrespective of the nature of transactions, we say that there is no exploitation. For example, if the employed person does not feel he or she is used and is happy with the remunerations in the realistic way, we say that there are no exploitations. The parents normally don't feel their children exploit them in spite of the fact they put enormous resources to bring them up.

Exploitation is a two way process. We cannot establish the exploiters and the exploited as a permanent attribute. For instance, when the employers and the employed are locked in a dispute about some issue, there is no telling beforehand which side will win. The fight is decided on each issue after both parties exhaust all the resources available for them. There is always some possibility that the winners and losers reverse the positions in the future when new developments take place within the organisation or in the society.

Exploitation can be a two way process in another sense. Two parties concerned may be exploiting each other at the same time. This view is more in line with the reality of life. This comes about from the nature of life: the employers needs the employed and vice versa. Within the family, the husband may dominate their wives and children, still the former must support the latter financially. Also the employers and the employed are mutually using the other: the former may exploit the latter through means of such as pay and empty promises; the latter may retaliate by means of such as work practices and sabotage.

It is harder to exploit single people than married people. Naturally this notion is revealed in the employers' preference to hire married people with children for professional positions. Single people may have the appearance of weakness since they are not backed by the family which is a fighting unit in the struggle for survival. However, I have been convinced through my experience of single life that the appearance is deceptive than real, although, admittedly, singleness is not always advantageous in dealing with varied businesses of life.

There is a financial advantage for the unattached people. Single people have to work, as a rule of thumb, only a few days a week instead of five days a week, to maintain the life style of a single-income family. If the former choose to work full time, they should be able to retire, if they wish, a long time before 65 years of age--45 in my case. Besides, in conjunction with money aspect, single people have mobility in both employment and residence, which they can use to the fullest extent, as the problems arise or their whims dictate.

Karl Marx's view of exploitation was widely off the mark of the real world. He asserted that the husbands exploited their wives and children within the establishment of family and also that the employers exploited the employees in the manufacturing environment. Nobody dispute the above assertion under specific circumstances. However, his serious mistake was that he thought the process of exploitation was inherent in the families and factories as they existed in his time. In reality, we must struggle for any gains tooth and nail on each issue and we cannot be sure of the immediate outcome, which, in turn, may change in any way in the future as the new developments take place.

The simplistic and unrealistic view on exploitation by Marx led to a wrong conclusion in relation to his communistic society he dreamed. He theorised that the capitalistic society made possible the exploitations he witnessed around him, as the previous social systems of slavery and feudalism did under the different setup. He offered a solution to the evil of exploitation; all forms of exploitation would cease if the new social system of communism came into existence and the state owned all production facilities within the national boundary. It is obvious to anyone who agrees with the principles of exploitation as I sketch in this section that the exploitations in modified forms must exist in the communistic society. In fact, the Russian people after the revolution of 1917 witnessed, to their horror, various forms of exploitations in their daily life.

Under the Third Prophecy, the exploitations still exist but become exceptions rather than the rules as we see today. Even today, the employers have a difficulty to exploit single people and in the future when the new philosophy becomes the way of life the exploitations will be hard to find. The exploitation within the family will not exist simply because single men do not have a family of their own: the thrust of the argument of this book is to lead people not to set up a family and not to have children. I am to deal with the topic of exploitation under the new society in the next chapter together with the other relevant themes.

Chapter 3 Manifestations of Third Prophecy

Section 1 General Survey

I am to disclose what impacts may await the individual who believes in the Third Prophecy at present and in the future. I am also to shed some light on the situation that may unfold if my doctrine is to prevail on a large number of people and this new philosophy is to dominate a society. Some critics would certainly argue that a substantial number of people would not believe in my proposition and hence the social impacts of the Third Prophecy are nonsense. I base my views in this chapter on my experience as a follower of the teaching coupled with my speculations. There is no documentary evidence to support my reasoning since no books have been published on the concept propounded in this book for all I know. I am to put forward the observations based on my experiences and also what I imagine the new society will be like. These speculations are not the main thrust of the new teachings which centre on the love of children by the individuals.

Though I sincerely believe that the new way of life will solve many of the serious social problems the humans are now having, I am prepared to face the following criticism. Some readers will point out simplicity of the solution I have offered may remind them of the fact that I denigrated Karl Marx for offering the simple solutions to the complex problems of the society. Some people may deride the simplicity of the essence of the Third Prophecy which, I say, will determine the future course of the human race. I like to remind readers that the human history has been formed by the ideologies--seemingly simple, though certainly theoretically and practically can be complicated--such as acquisition of necessities of life, sex, religion, idealism, materialism, racism, nationalism, sexism and arts. Any complicated philosophy which a few brainy people can understand has a limited impact on the fate of the humans as a whole. If a large number of people understand my simple philosophy with the consequent result, it has a vital significance on the future course of the human history.

I also anticipate some derision along the line of 'Having children or not is a matter for individual judgement, and philosophy cannot regulate or formulate it'. I am not going to build a new society. If a large number of people believe in my teaching, the new society will naturally emerge as a result and in fact it cannot be otherwise. A large number of books were written exploring religious and communistic doctrines and it takes us years to comprehend these theories expounded. However, once understood, I have found that these seemingly complex theories are not that hard and can be identified in our daily life. To counteract these critics who might say that I am a fool to make such an extravagant claim as to build a new society based on my way of thinking, this book emphasises that the previous prophecies were not totally correct as theories and do not fully explain the social phenomena both before and after their integrations into the human society. Only under the light of the Third Prophecy, our life and social phenomena make sense to my satisfaction and this teaching shows the way to social betterment, which is the topic of this chapter.

The Third Prophecy explains well what the society is like as we observe from our daily experience. It says that people become parents from lack of love. It further says that people do not love their children though they insist they do. Naturally we cannot expect these people to respect the rights of the children not of their own. Besides they spend their days looking after their children whom they fancy they love. Hence they don't hesitate to impinge upon life, liberty and the pursuit of happiness, which the Declaration of American Independence enshrined as unalienable rights of people. Neither do they respect liberty, equality and fraternity, which were the ideal of the French Revolution; nor whatever other high sounding ideals the students are taught at school. They do almost anything to try to obtain what they want though they are not entitled to, and try to escape due punishments. These attitudes come intrinsically to people who bring their children into this world for their own sake yet tell them they love them to their faces. Perhaps this is the best way to describe the state of the world to any growing up children who make the inquiry. Only the Third Prophecy gives the satisfactory answer to the query as to the nature of the society, because the new prophecy stands on the accurate vision of the true love rather than the views of such as religions and communism which do not fully explain the social phenomena.

Broadly speaking, the thrusts of my reasoning in this chapter are based on the following premises:

People, at the last stage of human evolution, have higher ethical standard, which will reflect in their daily life as well as in the social institutions of every kind, e.g., family, firm and government. People will not establish the families of their own and many of them may opt to live with their parents or siblings. People before the spread of the Third Prophecy were self-centred and did not care about their children, much less about the other people's children. Under the spell of the new philosophy, people will put the welfare of their unborn children first and will be concerned about that of the society they come under, and are to accept the teaching of 'Love thy neighbour' not only as a theory but as a daily experience. They also have ample time and energy to do their jobs conscientiously and thoroughly.

People who believe in the new way of life do not have families to support hence they don't have to lie and cheat to make a comfortable living as many people with families of the past and present have had to do. It is assumed that the government assist the temporarily or permanently disadvantaged singles. The society will have drastically reduced population, the degree of which depending on what percentage of people accepts the new way of life. The smaller number of people means an abundance of natural resources per capita, which people can use to the fullest extent without worrying about the environmental damages.

I would expect that the higher the educational standard, the higher the acceptance percentage of the new prophecy. Generally the better-educated behave less like animals and rely more on reason for judgement, thus making way for easier acceptance of love towards what exists only in the abstract mind. The above postulate matches with the demographic research. It is well established statistically that the rich have a smaller number of children than the poor. There is a general correlation between the levels of education and the income; hence the foregoing statistical statement is true about the educated and the uneducated.

Possibly idealism and materialism have no inherent defects as means for survival; however, people are unable to fulfil their ultimate aims of the two ideologies by the attitude of other people and circumstances and also by the fact that they have to share the resources with the other members of the family and the society. The problems of the world are neither in politics nor in social environment but rather a lot closer to heart. One social worker realised after many years of experience that the problems of the delinquent youths are in fact in the families and parents rather than in politics or society. I have the firsthand experience that the proper behaviours or misbehaviours of the children are directly traceable to the ways the parents treat their children properly or improperly.

Religion does not depend on the kind of society under which people live in order to reap the spiritual blessings. However, its moral codes are not in conformity with the worldly affairs and the faithful tend to lose in the struggles for existence. Many religious doctrines, realising this difficulty, emphasise the concept of life after death: The faithful will be rewarded and the sinful punished, not in this life but in the afterlife. Some faithfuls feel that the overall accounts of the good and evil deeds are not done in this life hence there has to be afterlife to balance the good and evil deeds of people. Communism uses similar tactics to religion in an effort to induce the believers to adhere to their teachings.

The communists can bring their claimed benefits to people only when the nation departs from the capitalist system and comes under the communist control. Many people who had genuinely believed in an ideal of classless and non-exploiting society died before the successful Communist Revolution in Russia. After the October Revolution of 1917 in Russia, many of the promises the revolutionary leaders made were not delivered: in fact, the revolutionaries found after the victorious revolution the statecraft was so different from what they had theorised that they did not even try to fulfil their varieties of commitments. Lenin admitted in 1922 that most of his government decrees issued in 1917 and 1918 were for propaganda purpose only and were not meant to be put into effect (Bradley 1988, p. 175). The people thus disappointed must have felt antagonism to the new regime. Objectively speaking, there is nothing surprising about the breaches of the promises made before the revolutionary outbreak since the public under capitalism are too often frustrated by breaches of election promises. When looked from the perspectives of benefits for people, the communist ideals, thus, can be said to be 'opium of the masses' or no better than flashy election promises.

I would imagine that the survival of human race is threatened by the following phenomena which are not independent but interrelated in a complex fashion:

- population explosion
- war
- spread of deadly diseases
- environmental degradation
- absolute or relative diminution of natural resources

Reduced population will effectively curb all of these problems. As a matter of fact, I cannot see any other solutions circulating such as technical innovations, promotion of friendly relations among nations, or better environmental policies backed by huge finance can be really effective in the long run. Hence I believe that from this angle too that the Third Prophecy must be the dominant belief for the welfare of the future human beings.

Unlike the past two major prophecies, the Third Prophecy brings immediate and lasting rewards to any individuals who follow and live up to its teachings, under any social conditions, irrespective of any religious beliefs. Next I disclose the general natures of the prophecy. I am to disclose in the section to follow independently of the general natures that the Third Prophecy which centres on love stronger than that between the sexes will solve the problems of war and woman. Men have agonised themselves through these evils since the immemorial times but have not even known the causes, let alone found the solutions. Then I am to disclose in the concrete forms the benefits and also a few shortcomings, one of which is quite serious, for these followers, first under the heading of 'Individually'. The section 'Socially' to follow is valid only when a significant number of people in one nation believe and practise the new teaching.

Section 2 What Third Prophecy Asserts.

Book One looks into idealism and materialism as we experience in our daily life.

Third Prophecy Does Not Assume a Particular Way of Life, Idealistically or Materialistically, except Perhaps Followers Remain Single.

Anyone under any social conditions may practise it: its adherence does not depend on religious or economic environment. The adherents can believe and support any religious and economic doctrines. All they have to do is to understand and agree with the teaching as I propound in this book and to have courage as small as a grain of sand to carry it through. In this sense the Third Prophecy is different from the previous prophecies whose main characteristic may be exclusiveness: Each tends to maintain that they are on the right and the others on the wrong. Buddhism and Christianity dogmatically maintained that their teaching was the whole truth and did not entertain any other thoughts. The communists fiercely attacked religion in general, and there was a time in Europe when the Catholics and the Protestants fought as if they were mortal enemies.

As the term 'Christian soldiers' and the song 'All ye warriors of God' imply, good Christians have to fight their way to maintain their faith. They have friends and foes in a similar way any other people, with or without a belief in a particular doctrine, have friends and foes. Certainly it is not the distinguishing quality of the religious to have enemies but it is the destiny of human beings, rather a fate of all living things. However, being the believers of the particular set of doctrines poses peculiar problems to them as for any other believers and non-believers have their own specific problems. The religious believers do not need any specific social conditions to follow their faith since the cardinal activities take place in their minds, though the religious environment in the society certainly help their social pursuits.

The communists tried to change the society into what, they believed, was right along the economic reasoning. They had certain specifications into which the society must conform. They exercised military insurrections backed by arguments and strikes to achieve the objective of transforming the society into the defined economic mould. The majority of the communists insisted that they could not bring about the communist society through democratic means.

Along the above reasoning, the communists are the worst off: they have the mammoth task of changing into their model the societies where so many dogmas of the varying fields are incessantly colliding. The religious people come next in the scale of difficulty: they have to maintain their faith in the course of friendly or hostile interactions with people of diverse beliefs. The followers of the Third Prophecy have the easiest task: all they need is a conviction which they can put into practice naturally, irrespective of their religious or economic beliefs.

In summary, the Third Prophecy is the simplest to understand and the easiest to perform; it will be shown in the subsequent pages it is the most effective to bring about a just and rich society. The concept is simple once understood but the today's generations and the people up to one century from now may have a difficulty in reaching to that understanding.

Third Prophecy Has No Supporting Theories as Religions and Communism Do.

All the Third Prophecy has is an unfailing love towards the children which is stronger than either self-love or love between men and women, and also a way how best people can express that love in practice, on the premise that satisfying physical and sexual needs belong to the different plane. In its essence it contains only love and nothing else. However, I am convinced that the Third Prophecy has the most profound effect on the life of the individual believers, and, if practised on a social scale, the greatest impact on that society. The simplicity of the aim is not confined to the Third Prophecy. If we step back and reflect the purposes of religions and communism, surprisingly we can express their aims in a few sentences. The vast literature written about these ideologies are supporting arguments and the means how to achieve the ultimate aims. Though we can define the religions in various modes, they are to serve people in explaining the mysteries of life and in giving the believers the spiritual truth. Christianity teaches that life is love which should be directed to the neighbours and ultimately to God. Buddhism teaches the doctrine of Mind Only (or Emptiness): life or the world is without any substance and hence is all illusions. The aim of communism may be to enforce the state monopoly of the means of production, thus eliminating exploitation and at the same time effecting the increased production. The complex supporting theories of religions and communism were developed to show people how to achieve the above aims. As far as the purposes are concerned, religions and communism are as simple as the Third Prophecy.

Third Prophecy Does Not Try to Persuade People to Follow Certain Course of Actions.
I do not wish that people choose my proposition: frankly I am careless. This new way of thinking reveals how best people can love their children. It further states how the human history is defective, and also propounds how these deficiencies can be corrected if people want to correct at all. In contrast with the above approach, the missionaries and communists in their zeal did their best to lead the public on the course which, they believed, were right spiritually or economically. The above two approaches may be compared to two methods of advertising. The former tells what products they have and leaves the consumers to decide. The latter tells what products they have and further goads the consumers to choose their brand.

People Who Follow Ideals of Third Prophecy Are Morally on Higher Level than Non-Believers.
This is obviously the law of large numbers if we can prove its correctness at all.

Being single all the life according to the Third Prophecy entails something more than happiness. This prophecy is beyond the considerations of happiness and unhappiness. The reasons of getting married, as I discuss in Section 5, Chapter 1 of this book, are more social convention rather than any particular reasons such as security, love between two sweethearts, economics with children, or sexual outlets. The reasons for having children, as I examine in the same section, are also attributable to social custom rather than identifiable reasons such as the sexual drive and the fear of death, and I dissect and analyse these social customs. Majority of people marry and have children, following the social convention and thinking that they will be happier. The fundamental idea about their children is that they are useful for them. We often hear that some married couples say that they like to have so many children. However, many pregnancies even within marriage are not planned and more to do with having sex without adequate preventative measures. Many unmarried girls get conceived simply because when they have sex they do not take precautions or do not have the knowledge of pregnancy. Also the females can get pregnant as a result of rape.

There are varied ways women get pregnant as outlined in the last paragraph. However, whatever reasons people put out for having the family of their issue, the decision of having the babies comes, to my way of thinking, from selfishness, even for pregnant girls as the result of rape. These people are self-centred and seeking fulfilment of their happiness, irrespective of that of the babies. As a consequence, as we expect from the natural or cosmic laws, they have a lot of problems within the family and do not normally achieve what they originally wanted, that is, their own happiness.

We cannot expect people who do not love their own children as I define to carry out the ethics such as 'Love thy neighbour'. People who believe in the Third Prophecy put welfare of their children above everything else, even being prepared to discard their own wellbeing. These people are not generally self-centred nor selfish to the extreme and accordingly they normally think and behave in an ethically higher mode than people who are acquainted with only the First and Second prophecies, that is, idealism and materialism respectively.

The First Prophecy states, 'Love your neighbour as yourself'. The Third Prophecy states, 'Love your children more than yourself'. Logically speaking, only when the latter is achieved, the former can be achieved. It is logically true and backed by my experience that 'Love thy neighbour' cannot be the rule of any society unless and until people learn to love their own children.

The parental burdens of bringing up children are due to the misconception about the nature of love towards their children. They don't love their children yet they say they do. The people who truly love their children as I am proposing are free from all cares associated with child rearing.

With the absence of the higher mode of thinking, idealism has been trampled down all these centuries. Idealists all over the world preached similar doctrines which centred in the concept of 'Love thy neighbour'. This essence of idealism naturally shows itself up as the following precepts:

Do not lie.
Do not steal.
Do not defraud.
Do not kill.
Seek justice

The states and religious institutions of selected societies of the world through the course of human history persistently preached people to conform to the idealist doctrines or the teachings of the sages possibly from their perceived gains, but fell far short of their objectives. The medieval churches in the West exclusively devoted to upholding the teachings of Jesus Christ. The examination system to recruit the government officials in the successive Chinese imperial dynasties centred on Confucianism.

The fact that the majority of people have ignored the above kernel of teaching whenever it suited them through the centuries can suggest a few possibilities:

- The propositions of the idealists are wrong.
- The humans by nature cannot accommodate idealism to their heart and make only lip service when it is advantageous.

I believe both of the above possibilities contradict human existence. Idealism promotes the welfare and harmonious life of the people. Idealism is what primarily set humans apart from animals. The human beings are capable of carrying out the propositions under the right conditions which will not exist up to the spread of the new philosophy as I propose in this book. The Third Prophecy is not about the common notion which states that unless people nurture well and give reasonable education, they should not bring children into this world.

A person tries to go up in a society in terms of wealth and reputation; however, as a rule people try to push down the person. This is natural since the loss of another is one's gain and people are ever jealous of another person's success. Because of these observations many people may insist that people won't change in this respect no matter what thinking is introduced into the society. Plato wrote: Every city is in a natural state of war with every other, not indeed proclaimed by heralds, but everlasting (Grant 1969, p. 137). Thomas Hobbes expressed the above human affairs as: For amongst masterless men, there is perpetual war of every man against his neighbour (Hutchins 1952, p. 114). Unlike Plato, Hobbes concluded that the human strife should cease if a sovereign with absolute authority governs people.

After the introduction of the Third Prophecy, idealism will have a fertile ground to bloom and mature despite the rationale of the last paragraph. Only after the ordinary people on the street learn how best they can love their children, is it expected they behave in a manner befitting to the ideals of the ancient sages: Love thy neighbours; seeking justice and treating the fellow humans as if they treat themselves, and doing their jobs with the utmost diligence. In the viewpoint of psychology too, people have to rely on their neighbours and friends for affection and love in the absence of their own family, hence they naturally promote the idea of 'Love thy neighbour' for their own good too.

It is logical to expect that only the perfect love of the Third Prophecy is capable of perfecting the previous prophecies. The Third Prophecy reaps the fruit of idealism--love and the fruit of materialism--material culture. Hence it stands to reason that the new philosophy can achieve so much while the previous philosophies, denying the other ways of thinking and the human achievements, achieved little of what they cherished.

In 'Introduction to Series' in Book One I assert that idealism (the First Prophecy) and materialism (the Second Prophecy) are two of the surviving strategies the humans devised through the course of development. The Third Prophecy completes these two means. Consequently an individual at present and a society in the future integrating this new prophecy command fully the fruits of the first two prophecies, and are the fittest to survive if abstractly expressed.

<u>Various Social (Political, Economic, etc.) Reforms Have Had Only Limited Impact on Any Society: Third Prophecy Has Capacity to Make Effective Reforms.</u>

Some people insist dogmatically all reforms were failures. However, if we look at the various nations, some nations, though they still may have serious problems, are better off than the others in many respects. Hence we can safely conclude that the efforts to better the society must have been successful in some nations than the others.

The social reformers, in whatever nation they may happen to live, who take the social reforms as their ultimate life goal, place the social welfare above their personal welfare, and despise people whose main concern is to establish themselves in their professions, will realise sooner or later that their efforts are fruitless and futile, and the job is beyond any person. This is also mostly true even with an everyday nuisance of various kinds. These people may in the end resign in the apathy concerning the reform. They may attribute the failure to the selfishness or egoism of the general public or to the nature of the human beings.

A good doctor diagnoses an illness to a specific cause such that it can be treated. If a doctor says the cause of the disease is the body type or nature, he is effectively saying he does not know how to treat it. If the medical science is further advanced, some disease, now incurable, may be treated effectively in the future. In the similar way I have come to the conclusion that the social reforms can be carried out effectively provided the specific conditions are met.

The incompetence in political and judicial systems has often been ridiculed in the mass media since it achieved wide circulation. It is true that there are many issues the decision makers have to take into account in dealing with the important decisions. They are in fact criticised for so obvious reasons that even the secondary school students can see the problems. The people ignorant of the Third Prophecy run these institutions. People who are capable of understanding this new philosophy are a new race or a member to the new party, distinct from the bulk of the population in the past and present. I call these distinct people the Third Race or the Third Kind. Only these people can perform the political and judicial systems effectively to the satisfaction of the people. Apart from the fact that these people are not only capable of understanding the higher mode of life but they are on morally higher ground and they have no need to care for their family.

We know that the successful reforms will eventually benefit the majority; hence the resistance to reforms must be really strong. One possibility is that the reformers do not have the correct theoretical background and represent only the small section of the community. Still I know that many reformers totally believed in their righteousness, though whether the observers can justify it is another matter. I say that the reasons for failures of the social reforms are specific and rooted in the ignorance of people in regard to the idea proposed in this book. Hence the social reforms, if well-conceived and skilfully executed, will most likely succeed in the atmosphere under the new philosophy. As an example of the above reason, the fitness for promotion in any organisation will be improved. Under the dominant force of the Third Prophecy, the fitness for the job will be the only criteria for the promotion, eliminating the room for Machiavellian to play tricks under certain circumstances today.

The concept of the Third Prophecy is very close to every human being and all have to make a decision to have children or not sooner or later in their life except for those who don't have any plans in life. It is this closeness and universality that I say it has a huge impact on human race unlike some excellent theories which are far removed from the ordinary people that they have small impact on a society. This reasoning matches with the teaching of the Bible: It [the commandment] is not in Heaven, ... Nor is it beyond the sea .... But the word is very near you, in your mouth and in your heart that you may do it (Deuteronomy 30:12-14).

People Will Receive Full Benefits of Idealism and Materialism.

In the course of human development, as I expand in Book One, one great achievement is idealism. Virtually all civilised peoples of the world have exhibited idealism in the various ways. The essence of idealism may be summarised in the teaching 'Love thy neighbour'. People who followed this teaching to the letter may realise, in the same way as the reformers may, that they cannot conduct the lesson in the real world except in exceptional circumstances. The teaching is not a rule in any society. We can infer that idealism did not have a total hold in any society from the fact, among other indications, that only an insignificant people remained single to uphold the idealism they cherished. Both in Buddhism and Christianity being single is an important teaching for the faithful not only in the monastery but in the ordinary household. This teaching comes from the fundamental premise of these religions. The Bible teaches that the attachment such as to marriage and family other than to God is an evil to avoid. The Buddha taught that everything, including marriage and family, is an illusion.

The conscientious and ethical people in an effort to realise what they cherish may come to the same conclusion as the reformers may. My research shows that there is nothing wrong with idealism. I say again that if the specific requirements are satisfied, the teachings will become the rule of the society, not the exceptions as they have been all these centuries. Until this requirement is met, that is, the wide diffusion of the new philosophy in the society, it is illogical to expect that the general public would behave in accordance with what the ancient sages preached.

In the sphere of materialism, the similar reasoning unfolds. In spite of the enormous development in the material aspect of civilisation, a large number of people in the world today still live in poverty. Even in the affluent society like Australia, there are many people whose living standards are not adequate for healthy and happy way of life. The average people in Australia must work hard for many years for descent material comfort, the absence of which is financially meagre life. We read in the Australian newspapers lots of frauds and swindles: the bottom line is that it is extremely hard to accumulate wealth with honest means. Here again the Third Prophecy opens up a new horizon not only for people who believe in the new way of life but for the fellow members of the society.

Materialism is the idea that material objects can solve many of our problems. Wealth is the command over the material, and consequent respect to the owners from the other people. We can obtain most of what we covet, certainly no all, using money. Materialism also manifests in scientific, technical, medical knowledge, and mass production of the commodities. The mass production creates wealth not only in the form of commodities, the profits for the shareholders and the wages for the workers but through the purchases needed for production. The profits and wages further increase the productive and commercial activities. Wealth can develop science and engineering, medical knowledge, superior armed forces and a host of the other scholarships.

Extending the metaphor of the disease and treatment further, I have postulated that we can liken the myriads of human problems to diseases and there are cures for many of the diseases. The medical treatments of social reforms, idealism and materialism were in the past only partially successful because they lacked the vital ingredient of love. The Third Prophecy with its uncontaminated love has to come to its aid for the treatments to be effective. Some readers may mock at the proposition but should refrain the judgement until they finish reading this book.

Upon learning the proposition of the Third Prophecy, the people whose interests are in the social reforms, idealism and materialism at present will wonder how stupid they were spending so much time and effort for such concepts, and will direct their mind to the new way of thinking proposed in this book. They will realise that what they wanted to see in the society will follow naturally and without efforts and conflicts, if the Third Prophecy prevails in the society.

Section 3 Cure from Wars and Women

I am writing this book from the general viewpoint; however, this section develops along men's point of view, emphasising that men not only took the lead in establishing marriage but had to go to war, and consequently agonised for all these millenniums. Men have to live with these two evils without any solution up to the arrival of the Third Prophecy. Besides, the topic of this section stands on its own separate from the others. This section concerns itself only with women in the domestic context and not in the occupational capacity. Men have a choice to marry or not but do not have a choice dealing women in the occupational capacity. Besides men have universally adverse opinion about women in the domestic situation but they have diverse opinions concerning women' occupational capacity.

Women are similar to hard drugs to men though many men do not seem to know this assessment. Both give men intense pleasure as well as acute suffering, yet most men strive to obtain beautiful women, and some, hard drugs. Both take their heavy toll in finance and emotion, but men still feel they have to have women and some, drugs.

Average men are not addicted to heavy drugs and these men do not understand why the drug addicts sacrifice so many other things in life in an attempt to acquire a tiny amount of the desired drug. All good parents would wish their children to keep away from hard drugs. Still they don't warn their sons to keep away from the females. One reason may be, judging from their own experience, no amount of warning would be effective in the light of the strong male sexual drive. Carefully assessed, perhaps the females would inflict as much damage on the youths as hard drugs would over the years. A strange thing about this attachment to womenfolk is that the youths do not learn any lessons from their observations. They normally have an ample opportunity to learn what women and marriages are like from what they see around them--the families of their own as well as of the acquaintances and in the neighbourhood. Most boys form a negative opinion about the opposite sex and marriage and often express that in the open, yet in maturity as soon as they find good and agreeable girls they are eager to get into cohabitation--married or unmarried. Incredibly many divorced men, who were hurt and suffered tremendously through marriage, still seek women for cohabitation after a healing period.

I would say that sexual love blinds men in a similar fashion euphoria, the drug addicts: both groups of people lose control of themselves. Men, in an effort to satisfy their desire for the females, as the drug addicts for the drug, take the plunge into matrimony regardless of the consequences. Single youths need more than conventional wisdom to remain bachelors and lead a higher and better mode of life. A contrived aphorism such as if people remain single they will be happier is of little use against the strong sexual drive. I have written this book to help them achieve what started for the welfare of their children but will result in their boon. I sometimes get to know a woman through the course of my life, feeling what a terrible life her husband may be having. I feel disgusted knowing her only for a short time and her husband must put up with her day in and day out with no end in sight.

A poet in ancient Greece read a poem: 'Wars and women are necessary undying evil'. It is not hard to make a comment from the personal experience but the poet's high intelligence is revealed in his insight that wars were necessary, which was beyond his immediate grasp. Euripides wrote, 'Yea, own women's nature 'tis--say they--to be most helpless for all good, but fashioners most cunning of all ill' (Harbottle 1897, p. 347). Simonides of Amorgos wrote, 'No greater evil Zeus inflicts than women' (p. 381). I am sure that a large number of men, past and present, would agree with the spirit of the above verses which the poets learned from their bitter experience. Since men excluded women from professional jobs in the ancient to classical Greece as in any other parts until the modern times, the poets were referring to cohabitation with women and not their professional competency.

The following passages come from Latin sources. Write me in air, or in the flowing stream, a woman's vows to a too ardent lover [Catullus] (p. 140). Women have many faults, and of the many, this is the chief: delighted with themselves, too great a zeal they have to please the men [Plautus] (p. 141). Dust is lighter than a feather, and the wind more light than either; but a woman's fickle mind more than feather, dust or wind [Davison's Poetical Rhapsody] (p. 237). Lighter than falling leaves are women's words, and nothing worth; the sport of winds and waves [Ovid] (p. 300). Not hard for thee to fashion words and wiles. This art has every woman made her own [Propertius]. (p. 307)

I heard many times that women were as good as men professionally and also l heard many comments that women were not very proficient from the occupational viewpoint. I am not sure how to pass the judgement on this matter but in any case I am dealing with women in the domestic situation. Wars and women have been something men have not learned to live without in spite of their harsh involvements through the millenniums. The foregoing poets and the majority of men are not aware that they can live without these two evils, provided they get to know how reading this book.

Not all ancient Greeks looked at war as evil. For example, the poet Hesiod said that strife was wholesome to men. He further said that the victory of war brings wealth to his city state, though he did not elaborate what happened to his state if it lost the war and also the sufferings of people, combatants and civilians, through battles. There are also abundance of poetry extolling the love between men and women, which I do not have to quote since readers are familiar with, I am certain, under the various contexts.

Wars on the national level are like the important examinations on the individuals. The victors of the war are assured of the power over the losers in the same way the qualified people are assured of the privileges. Both test the endurance of the average people to the limit, though it is true that a nation can have an easy victory of war and there are a small number of brainy students who can pass the examinations with ease. Dreaming of the good result, many people are ever eager to win the war and pass the examinations, putting all the efforts under their sleeves. Failure to do so ends up in a disappointment and misery often for the rest of their lives.

Many people voice strong objections against waging a war but these people should know that it is just as hard for a nation to live without wars as for men to live without women or without any troubles in their daily life. In fact it is easier for people to solve the problem of overpopulation or many other problems by war. Possibly when men learned to live without women, the nations, which men had dominated in the past, would have learned to live without wars.

Men who say that they would rather have women than wars do not take into account of the percentage of men engaged in war as well as of the time frame. We know that from the ancient times to the present, it was generally the case that only a small percentage of men who were young, healthy and strong engaged in battles. A war, if fierce, normally does not last longer than a few years and besides there are some reliefs from war duty for the individuals on leave. Women, on the contrary, can be with men year after year without breaks. So I would say that wars and women are twin evils either of which can be deadly to men in different ways.

I believe that when the Third Prophecy becomes the dominant ideology in many advanced countries of the world, there is no need for a nation to wage a war on another nation. In fact it is virtually impossible for these countries to start a war since massively reduced populations mark these converted nations, though I am not assuming here that the overpopulation is the only cause of wars. As a matter of fact before the Neolithic era, when the population was sparsely scattered, there was no evidence that the humans fought wars constantly.

Let us look at the recent example of the Iraq War. Most likely the fundamental reason why the US forces attacked Iraq was the serious concern of future oil supply not only for the US but for the world. The estimates of the proven oil reserves in 2011 from OPEC, CIA World Factbook, oil companies: for Iraq 8.9% and for the United States 1.4% versus the total oil reserves of the world. The stated reasons by the American President Bush of the possession of mass destruction and the prevention of terrorist attack are hardly convincing. The lack of oil supply is the critical problem for the Americans; thinking it as the survival issue thus the president sent the armed forces to Iraq in 2003 amid the fierce oppositions around the world. A few other plausible reasons were put forward by the eminent people. Even all these views were correct, if the demographic forecast was the drastic population decrease for the United States in the near future, for example, as a result of the prevalence of the Third Prophecy, I would bet that the war did not eventuate.

This section and this book for that matter, concerns itself with only the obvious ways of preventing wars and does not try to delve into the complicated or specific causes of wars. However, I have noticed some relationships between the personal conflicts and the wars at the national level. Wars to the state are similar to the various conflicts to the individuals. We, the individuals, can be put in a position where we have no choice but to start a personal war for social existence, honour, money or whatever else we cherish. For example, if someone or organisation insults us or deprives us of certain rights, we justifiably feel we must go on a personal war, sometimes risking everything we have.

When things around get upper hands on us, we think and behave in a fit of anger in an attempt to solve the problems. This same frustration projected among the nations, I believe, is one of the seeds of wars. When a group of people cannot solve their differences amicably, they often quarrel and even exchange blows, which is another seed of national wars. At the time of conflicts, we often see the true state of affairs that have been covered up either in the recess of the minds or in the interpersonal relationships. So, in this light, war is in fact something which has to happen if we want to understand the truth of our minds or the interpersonal relationships. After the war the two nations as for the two individuals get to know what the adversaries are, and sometimes they become good friends and sometimes they become mortal enemies.

When there is a problem in individuals, families, firms and nations, there are many issues and life views emanating from the survival instincts. People involved are often not aware what are the fundamental problems are and they have contradicting views within themselves.

One reason why people have conflicts is that people have the different life or world views depending on what they choose as their survival techniques. For example, an individual who is convinced of religious doctrines may try to preach them in his eagerness but he often gets into strife with the people holding different survival techniques. Further many nations which were proud of the religious righteousness engaged in the military conquests to spread the belief on the assumption that only the military victory would force the change of the life views of the unreligious.

When there is a dispute between two nations, the general rule is that the dispute should be settled in proportion to the relative strengths--economic, political and military--in the international arena rather than the justice which is the domain of idealism. If the two nations do not agree about their relative strengths, they have a serious problem at hand.

One source of conflict or war is that the two parties do not agree with the relative worth or strength. For example, a person in a firm may not have the right concept about its worth. The firm management may think the person is not worth that much and may try to ignore its rightful request. The positions people hold in a firm does not fully reveal what they are worth. Conflicts and wars are like earthquakes and they are adjustments.

One major search of the humans is to know what we are, as Socrates taught people to know themselves. When there is a misconception in us, which can develop into conflicts, whose consequences often tell us what we really are.

The disputes among the individuals are mainly decided by brain power, wealth, social status, acquaintances or the physical strength, shown or exercised. Similarly, the disputes among the nations are chiefly decided by the political, economic or military strength, constantly shown and sometimes exercised. The military might exercised is what we call war.

There is a fundamental correlation between wars and personal conflicts. The large population in a nation has similar effect as the large family in that both deprive the resources of the people in the respective group. Apart from the foregoing premises, it is widely believed that the population pressure is the underlying cause of wars. The natural reasoning from this thinking is that it is a good policy not to increase the population density such that we don't confront the serious problem of shortage of resources such as land and mineral deposits. Once the population reaches to a certain level; naturally the people who favour the war solution for the various problems would dominate politics. These people would support the notion to start a war, thus killing unwanted people and also conquering another territory for the surplus population to migrate. Whatever causes of wars we may assign for our intellectual satisfaction, that does not help us much since wars have been an ever present menace throughout the human history after the agriculture came into existence, as is clearly evidenced by high defence budgets and high preparedness of virtually all nations on earth at present.

The similar reasoning can apply to women and marriage; I am presenting the way the ordinary people can live without marriage. Without cooperation of husbands and wives the bringing up the babies is not economically sustainable for most people unless they receive the government help. In the past the government help was not available hence the husbands and wives had to cooperate to bring up the children and the number of births out of wedlock was statistically small compared with that within marriage. Today marriage is not an economic unit in the sense it used to be with the government assistance in the economically advanced countries. If most people do not marry, naturally that leads to vastly reduced population in that nation even with the government assistance available, which in turn leads to the high probability that the nation does not have to start a war. The majority of people want to have babies within marriage.

I have come to understand that breaking up of the firms, nations and empires is essentially no different from the breaking up of the families, though the reasons and how it happens may be different in each case. These human institutions break up when the people in them feel these institutions are useless in terms of finance, emotion and sex. In the firms, nations and empires finance, and emotion in some situation, are the main focus of concern; in the families money, emotion and sex are stressed. If abstractly expressed, these human institutions come into existence when the people think they are useful for their survival and pleasure, and cease to exist when people judge they are useless for their survival and pleasure.

Remedies for Twin Evils of Wars and Women

Switzerland has not experienced a war to speak of in the past two centuries. The French defeated the Swiss in Italy in 1515 and the Swiss began their policy of permanent neutrality. In 1798, during the French Revolution, French armies swept into Switzerland and quickly occupied the country. In 1815, the Congress of Vienna restored the old confederation, expanded Switzerland to 25 cantons adding three cantons and guaranteed Swiss neutrality.

Today there are 20 cantons and six half-cantons in Switzerland. Only one canton Jura entered the confederation in 1974: This is the only additional canton after the decision of the Congress of Vienna. From these figures we can conjecture how Switzerland has been stable politically since 1815, though there have been squabbles. The Swiss neutrality has never been broken since then, though there was a brief, lasting only 25 days, civil war in 1847. Since 1848, there was an absence of major internal crises along ethnic and religious lines. With political stability it has prospered, developing industry, agriculture and communication.

It possesses at present a highly efficient defence force equipped with the precision weapons manned by diligent and efficient personnel. Switzerland has a militia (citizens' army) instead of regular armed forces.

The governor of New Zealand signed the Electoral Act of 1893, heralding the first female suffrage in the world. Virtually all economically advanced nations of the world allowed the participation of women in politics as both candidates and voters in the 20th century.

For more than 700 years Switzerland has maintained the world's oldest and one of Europe's most effective democracies, achieving an exceptionally high standard of living (*Encyclopaedia Britannica*, 15th edn, sv, Switzerland.). In one canton and in four of the half-cantons, the people vote by a show of hands at an open-air meeting. However, Switzerland was the last major European country to grant women political equality. In 1958, Basel became the first Swiss city to allow women to vote in local elections. In 1971, women in Switzerland were given the right to vote in national elections. National referendum in 1971 amended the constitution to grant women the right to vote in federal election and hold federal office.

The cantons, regional political units, followed the suit and allowed the female participations in politics. However, Appenzell Inner-Rhoden, a half-canton, does not allow the female participation in politics even today. This half-canton still carries on the open-air political meetings by the show of hands, that is, direct democracy. The population of this half-canton was 13 000 in 1985 and the bulk of the people are German speaking and Roman Catholic.

These two events, that is, barring the females from politics and absence of wars, are mere coincidences and have no correlations. Before the twentieth century, practically all the nations of the world barred women participating in political activities, yet virtually all these nations engaged in incessant wars. So keeping women out of politics does not help prevent wars.

The patients (most men) who are afflicted with the evils of war and woman can learn from the curing technique of the nervous problem outlined in Section 7, Chapter 1. The sufferers of the nerves wrongly look at the symptoms of the problem for solution and do not understand that the cure must come from somewhere else other than the manifestation. Similarly the sufferers of the twin evils think that they can get rid of these evils by simply attacking them head-on. Some men openly object to wars and join the street demonstrations but the wars are still with them. Many men speak ill of women and some even bash their wives, still these men cohabit with women for whatever reasons they may have.

Arthur Schopenhauer, German pessimist philosopher, thought that women were inferior and did not marry all his life. However, he was an exception to the rule: men in general cannot keep away from women for long because of their strong sexual drive. Switzerland has not had a war with any other country for the last two centuries; however, this fact is also an exception to the general rule and has more to do with geography than anything else.

The Swiss Alps are part of the mighty Alps, the largest mountain system in Europe, and covers about 60% of Switzerland. It was also helped by the strong pride in freedom and independence by the Swiss who consist of German, French, Italian and Romansh. The cousins of the first three nationalities in the respective homelands engaged in the incessant wars; the origins of the Romansh speaking people is unclear. Another contributing factor may be lack of mineral resources, the abundance of which would have induced the neighbouring nations after industrialisation in the 18th and 19th centuries, to occupy and utilised the resources to their advantage. Neutrality of Switzerland gave Hitler an assurance that the Swiss would not enter the war on the side of the Allies; hence his army did not invade Switzerland at the beginning of World War II. There was no doubt that if Switzerland had had vast oil reserves which Hitler desperately wanted, the Hitler's army would have invaded and occupied the land as a first priority. Belgium was a neutral country prior to World War Two but the Hitler's army overran the country on the way to France. This was the geography in conjunction with the French defence line.

Another contributing factor for the Swiss not to have engaged in war is also geography in conjunction with race. Germany, France and Italy surround Switzerland. The peoples from these countries form the bulk of the Swiss population hence it is hard for the Swiss to start a war with their cousins.

Poland was attacked through the centuries primarily because of its position between the Teutonic race and the Russians: the Russians are the East Slavic race and the Polish, the West Slavic race. The armies of either Russia or Germany must occupy this region with the access to the Baltic Sea, with the sea acting as the routes of supplies and interceptions, before they can proceed any further. When the German army invaded Poland on the first day of September 1939, its intent was obviously the preparatory step to attack Russia. Accordingly Britain and France immediately declared war on Germany. Stalin did not think in the same way and was unprepared for the imminent German invasion into Russia, though certainly he had been aware that major war was coming and Russia had been geared for the development of heavy industries, particularly armament industries, and the armed forces. In fact the German forces invaded Poland in line with the secret protocol of the Molotov-Ribbentrop Pact signed by Molotov and Ribbentrop in Moscow on 23 August 1939. The Bolsheviks, just after their successful revolution in Russia, wanted to occupy Poland as a stepping stone to Western Europe. Its failure put paid to further conquest in Europe and its expansive drive was to be directed to the Third World.

The solution to the problem of war and woman does not come from the logical reasoning about the subjects. Humans are not really logical in their thinking and behaviours as we might hope. The ancient Greeks with all their marvellous wisdom could not devise any solutions to the problems. The majority of the Greek men married and had to engage in the constant war activities with the neighbouring (Greek and foreign) states. Even Socrates, a sage, engaged in battles. We may postulate that it is not wisdom but love which offers the answer. Judging from this perspective, love is in higher order than wisdom and is more fundamental than wisdom to humans. Christianity whose major feature is love has had deeper and wider influence over the European civilisations before the modern era than the Greek philosophy whose main concern was truth, justice and beauty. However, it was not in the Christian tradition to condemn wars and women. Certainly the Christians through the ages urged people to be single such that they can concentrate on the Christian way of life; however, it did not use love as the basis of singleness. Hence, Christianity did not contribute to the removal of these evils though, possibly, the ideology based on love if properly directed was capable of doing so.

Average men need more subliminal thinking than the considerations of happiness and wealth to keep away from women in the domestic context. The cure of nervous problems does not come from the willpower of the patients; in the same way the cure from women does not come from the willpower of the suffering men either. The nervous attacks for people with nerves, and the acquisition urges for women--sex is one reason and affection is another--of ordinary men are such strong forces that they simply cannot resist. The Third Prophecy whose essence is love is in fact the answer for not marrying women. The cure from the nerves must come from the proper growth of the defective brain. In the same way the cure from women must come from the proper thinking of love which the Third Prophecy introduces. Nothing else can remove the average men of the sufferings coming from the nervous and female problems. The force of these curing techniques on the patients is in fact stronger dictate than willpower.

Average men, if imbued with love stronger than the love between the sexes as defined in the Third Prophecy, can stay out of family life, in order not to have children. That is possible because they do what is best for their children whom they love dearly rather than what is best for themselves. Certainly the teaching of the prophecy does not root out from men the sexual desire: it does not remove men of the constant urge for women. Single men with the sexual problem should peruse Book Five *The Sexual Laws* to have better understanding of sex and to find the solution of the problem. However, no women in the domestic context, and no wars if adopted by the bulk of men, are the minor by-products of the Third Prophecy whose chief message is love of children as I define.

Section 4 Individually

All persons who follow the Third Prophecy will receive the following consequences; mostly good and some adverse. The deep affection towards our own children rather incredibly leads to the various benefits. Hence I call the Third Prophecy truth.

People feel love towards their children, though non-existent in the physical world, all their life without hurt feelings. They have the conviction that they have accomplished something great which they do not want to exchange for anything else in the world. The love I am advocating will be the strongest, purest and lasting for life people will ever know in their life; they will be prepared to sacrifice everything else they have including their sweethearts.

This is the most important and primary benefit for the people who believe in the new philosophy as I expound in this book. The kernel of the Third Prophecy is love and also happiness emanating from that emotion. This book is dedicated to convey the sense of that love to the general public using various means since it is extremely hard to express love of any forms on paper.

The following speculations are incidental and some are true even to the people who don't want to leave offspring in this world from other reasons than love of my definition, and also to the people who want but cannot have babies from various reasons. If people base the decision to be single all their life on happiness consideration, these people may decide to marry when they feel unhappy since all people have a cyclic experience of happiness and unhappiness.

The believers of the new philosophy do not marry. The believers have no family of their own to care for financially and one thousand other ways: they can do whatever they like in their life to be free from many worries of married people with children. They may opt to live with their parents, siblings or friends.

Single people may give the impression that they are vulnerable to be taken advantage of. As my experience goes, this is more apparent than real and they can take the upper hands in most struggles in life.

Single people have little motivation to exploit other people: particularly the believers in the new philosophy with high ethical level do not have much interest in using people on the way to get what they want.

It is also harder to exploit unmarried and mature persons than people married with children, or younger, or older people. Single people with many years of job experience tend to conduct themselves at home as well as at work in an overbearing manner which comes naturally from being free in many ways. The employers may not like this attitude and may appoint married men or married women for responsible positions. In other words, the organisations may prefer married people with children to single people for jobs with considerable responsibilities, since the former tends to yield than the latter more easily from the management pressures which come to all professional people, whether married or not. I am quite certain that this is not the case for unimportant and unprofessional jobs. Generally speaking, as my observations go, many organisations, particularly if they are small, tend to appoint professional people with some weakness such that they can be used to the ultimate gains for the organisations. Married people with children have a weakness in that they have to support the family and are reluctant to fight with the employers even when they feel they are on the right. The practice of appointing married people for professional positions is widely spread but rarely talked about because the decision makers leave that out from the assessment, knowing that the preference to the married people for any position is against the law in virtually all advanced countries of the world. We can say the same thing about nationality, age and sex of the applicants.

Single people, especially men, may have a difficulty in finding sexual outlet. The new teaching does not object that men have sex with girlfriends or prostitutes with the extreme precaution against pregnancy and transmission of diseases, or opt for masturbating.

<u>How I Wrested Retrenchment Money from Government--Instance of Reverse Exploitation.</u>
This episode is a good example how a single man can take upper hands in the struggle for existence, belying his apparent weakness. I am sure that had I been married with children, the course of events would have been entirely different and I would have been the receiving end rather than the leading figure of the fight. The development as well as the result of the fight decided the issue of who exploited whom. Singleness is not necessarily advantageous in dealing with the myriads of events in life in the same way beautiful girls find on some occasions their beauty is not advantageous, and the rich men find on some occasions their wealth is not advantageous. This story has been chosen because the situation I was in was of a kind which an average person would have got into in his or her life. I have had a lot fiercer and harder fights in the past than this story tells.

I had in my life many fights as the ordinary people would: In many cases they were thrust upon me. I had the fiercest struggle in my raw youth, putting everything I had on the line. If I had lost, I would have literally lost everything and I would not have been in a position to retire at the age of 45 and devote my time on book writing. On one fight I had to rely on my sheer patience. The enemies were too strong and if I had opted to fight I would have lost. By sheer patience I came out well as a total winner. People expected I would lose and did not interfere into the affair. These onlookers were really surprised to witness my attackers went down with serious consequences lasting for the rest of their life. On rare occasions I had to resort to my physical strength to win over the opponents. On rare occasions I had to resort to the dirty tricks which would have constituted offences punishable by laws, though they were strictly limited to my retaliation to the wrong doings done on me. In all the struggles I went through after acquiring religious teachings, I realised that I could interpret all of them by the religious theories including the fight I lost: I lost the fight because I acted against the teachings I had cherished.

My job in the public service seemed quite secure as was expected working as a permanent staff with two engineering qualifications. Also my finances were as good as an average single person of 44 years of age can hope under the normal circumstances. However, I had one serious problem that had persisted almost half of my life up to that time: I did not like what people call engineering and also hated to work in any organisation. My way of thinking was formed by literature which I loved reading since I was a little boy. I read a large number of books, mainly on history, classical literature and also after adolescent on religion. I think only sex held a similar degree of fascination to me. When I was studying to become an engineer, I had a difficult task of learning technical approach, though in the end I acquired two engineering degrees by sheer perseverance. After a few years of painful adjustment to my way of thinking since obtaining the second degree, I managed to secure an engineering position in a private firm. It was easy to get a position in the government munitions factory after a short experience in the above company. I was delighted to work in the munitions industry which had some kind of fascination to me. Having worked in the munitions factory with all my diligence for a few years, I acquired high degree of expertise, which was naturally conveyed to me by various means as would happen in any organisation.

I said to myself that my life in the public service was good and even tried to like engineering by reading technical books. To try to like what one does not like is not done often, and rarely is it successful. I did not change an iota as far as the dislike of engineering was concerned but I acquired engineering competence.

My problem apart from dislike of engineering started with the wrong attitude or policy within the public service. If the public service had had the policy concerning the transfer and promotion as I outline in the next paragraph, I would not have had any problem in the public service and probably stayed there until I retired.

One serious problem in the government of any country as I understand is that the managers or the heads of the sections do not want to transfer competent and hardworking people under them to another department or section. The good workers tend to be used, though people may speak well of them. They are willing to transfer incompetent and lazy workers. Consequently the good workers do not get the experiences to be promoted in the future. The setup should be the other way around. The government is capable of developing a policy such that the good workers get transferred as soon as they know enough to do the jobs, and the bad workers should be kept in the same jobs. Certainly the transfer goes against the interests of the managers and section heads under whom the good workers work: however, the policy should make a provision to override the objections. The policy is also enforced for the interests of the good workers, the public service as a whole and the nation. If the policy is well entrenched with successful records, many people will put out their best performances to be transferred and to be promoted with more salary. As it is, the incoming workers, they may be well motivated at first, learn quickly that it is not worth working hard and become lazy and incompetent after a while. They may listen intently to the problems in the public service from the officers and management, but they often don't lift a finger to try to solve the problems.

After working in the same factory for eight years, my life became increasingly boring and difficult, the initial fascination with the weapons wearing thin and the disinterest in the engineering taking the upper hands. Minor adverse happenings easily irritated me. I had been thinking of a plan for a few years by that time to devote my time in writing a book whose idea I had conceived more than 20 years earlier. In fact this is the book I am referring to. I was seeking a way out and an opportunity for change presented itself.

Though I was stationed in the Industrial Engineering section at the time, I did virtually no works of that section. The development of commercial stores assigned to me were almost complete by that time, and the plant commissioning job occupied most of my working hours. My supervising manager (Engineer Class 4) was so impressed with the progress of the commissioning which had been big thorns on his side for quite some time prior to my taking charge that he agreed to promote me to Acting Engineer Class 3. I had found at the commencement of the project that the designation of commissioning was a facade to hide the management embarrassment. The project was far from the commissioning stage, though many people had a go at it over the years. It was agreed between the two that the new arrangement would last until the following year when the major organisational change was to take place, hence 'acting' was to be attached to my new position indicating both that the position was not permanent and that I would be on that position temporarily.

However, this manager was not a member of the Executive Committee and had to do my promotion business through his supervising manager (Engineer Class 5). This Executive Manager repeatedly ignored the recommendation for my promotion, not telling my immediate supervisor the reasons for non-concurrence and also that he had had a bitter fight with me a few years earlier. Nor did I tell anybody of the fallout and I was sure that nobody else knew about it. The enmity between us was so strong that either of us would have attacked the other with a slightest pretext. I had better reason to be careful about him than he about me because his ranking in the organisation was a lot higher than mine. He was Engineer Class 5 and I was Engineer Class 2: the salary ratio was 1.3 to 1 but the authority difference was far greater than the salary ratio indicated.

The social convention states that if the employer mistreats the employee, the latter is supposed to resign to maintain the dignity; if the employee misbehaves the employer has to dismiss the former to maintain the good standard of the organisation. But I knew better than quitting the job when the manager insulted me concerning my transfer: it may be more appropriate to say that I was not ready to leave. I waited for a chance to retaliate and hit at the Executive Manager in the future. This is a good example to show that patience is a virtue.

We often do not tell people the extreme emotions of such as love or hate, thinking that the words uttered are not adequate to express the emotional state and also hiding these emotions within ourselves from some other reasons. That was the mode I and possibly the Executive Manager were in.

The patients with extremely painful experience tend not to talk about the experience. I was nowhere near being called a patient and I simply chose not to tell anyone about it. Therapists encourage the patients with post-traumatic stress disorder to talk about their experience in order to view them objectively and to reduce the pains. This process is called Catharsis in psychotherapy.

A few months passed with this stalemate. I was not worried about the non-progress of my promotion at all: the extra money for higher duty was so small that the promotion was hardly worth worrying about and in fact a small number of the public service staffs declared that they did not want promotions. I owned two houses at the time and the rents from these houses were a lot more than the extra money for Class 3 job; in fact, my total income was as much as the General Manager's salary.

Around this time I received the confidential information which stated that the factory would lay off a fair number of the employed at the reorganisation of the following year (1989). This piece of knowledge was in direct contradiction to the public statement of the General Manager that there would be no retrenchment at the reorganisation. I then resolved to try to obtain the retrenchment money, betting that some people would be retrenched.

First I made it an open knowledge that I intended to retire from the professional job such that I could devote my time writing a book. Then I started preparing for a new life, financially, professionally and emotionally as a writer. This was in the middle of the year and the reorganisation was expected in April, the following year.

When I made myself clear that I was going to leave the public service, I stopped all the commissioning work which was my major task at the time. I hoped that it would not only enhance the probability of being laid off but would enrage the Executive Manager earlier mentioned. I was prepared to place the blame on him for my stopping the project, though my underlying reason was to obtain the retrenchment package. I had been seeking a chance of revenge on him for the previous few years, not being content with an insult I had delivered on him, but had not been able to find any other means until this opportunity. Stopping the project was meant to be an insult on him who had insulted me before in conjunction with my transfer. The internal inquiry would have revealed that the Executive Manager was in fact blocking my promotion if not the earlier insult I had received, which would have made the management reluctant to take any punitive action on me. The recommendation of my promotion by a manager would not have necessarily resulted in the actual promotion but the management at least had the duty to respond in some way or another. I believed that this oversight embarrassed the management.

Being single with no children possibly make people unforgiving when they receive slurs or insults. The married people with children may carry the grudge in their minds under the same treatment, but there is nothing much they can do about it and may opt to forgive and forget, which the affection on their children accelerates, though this affection may be misguided in my opinion as I stated earlier in this book.

I needed a small time to finish off the commercial store at hand and had to change only the parameters to suit the similar store the order of which the government obtained from the private industry around this time. Though I had the authority to pass the remaining job to the production department needing only a small input of time and effort at that stage, it was tactically important for me to carry them through. In the first place this arrangement sent a message to the management that the problem was in the commissioning and not in the commercial projects. In the second place, if I had stopped all the jobs, the managers could have proved that I did not do any work which could have made me liable to dismissal: the managers could not have established how much time I put into the commercial projects in the Sales Department, as long as I kept working. The dismissal, though it meant nothing to me in itself, would not have given me the package I wanted. In the third place, stopping the commissioning only would have made the Executive Manager seething: I ignored the commissioning in retaliation for ignoring my advancement. Stopping the commissioning was effective in another sense. The project was fast approaching a meaningful conclusion under my care and the managers would have had a serious problem of finding the replacement as had been the case before my appointment. I spent the spare time, learning English, talking with the colleagues and walking around the huge ammunition factory.

In the Federal government in Australia, at that time anyway, it was extremely difficult to dismiss the permanent staffs holding the designated positions; however, the government changed the rules on dismissal after 1989. My position was attached to the commercial stores and not to the Industrial Engineering, nor to the commissioning jobs. One method to effect dismissals was to prove a case of misconduct. Another was to abolish the positions belonging to the staffs. In fact the retrenchments in all the public services in Australia, the local, the states and the commonwealth, were done through abolishing the designated positions. I was fully aware that the commissioning job did not exist on a permanent basis and I suspected that the Executive Manager might use that fact to block my promotion. Had he used that excuse at all, he would have effectively recommended me for retrenchment in the due course of time. My appointment on another job at the changeover, particularly if the position offered to me was only Class 2 Engineer for I had proved myself capable of doing higher duty, would have given me additional ammunition to fight further instead of resigning since the non-existence of the commissioning work on a permanent basis was the ample reason for my being laid off.

Naturally I adopted the policy of not disclosing why I discontinued the commissioning. In the course of stalemate lasting for 9 months, the management of the factory pulled a trick on me. It came through as a disguised phone call to me. I believed that the caller wanted me to say what the true intent behind my inaction was. If I had said that it was an attempt to get the retrenchment money, it would have constituted a clear case of misconduct proven and I would have been dismissed straightaway irrespective of what the Executive Manager had done to me a few years earlier as well as ignoring the recommendation of my promotion. I also suspected that the management was probing if they offered me an acting Class 3 position, I was prepared to do the commissioning. As a matter of fact the promotion at this time would have deprived me of the moral justification to fight on; the promotion did not suit my ultimate purpose. Stopping the commissioning job itself did not make sufficient reason for dismissal because the job did not belong to me as the public service act designated. I made a reply in such a way to make them feel that the trick of that nature simply did not work on me that they never tried again. At the same time any chance of my being appointed as acting Engineer 3 disappeared.

I still don't know what line of reasoning was used to reach the decision but the fact of the matter was that I was to be retrenched at the time of the reorganisation according to the factory notice. I might have been laid off even if I had not played any tricks since the Sales Department was to be closed. Perhaps in this case the thinking behind was not important but only the fact that I got the package which I desperately wanted mattered, in the same way it does not matter how the lottery winner selected the winning number and only the winning counts.

I cannot even assess the implications of stopping the commissioning job. The management in the public sectors as in the private sectors do not disclose as a rule how they arrived at a particular decision. Possibly they want the monopoly in decision making, minimising the interferences from the employed. Some people adversely affected by the decision may try to reverse the decision if the reasons offered are incorrect. If no reasons are given there is nothing much the dissatisfied people can do. I also can surmise that if something goes wrong after the decision, which happens sometimes, the victims are left in the dark as to who was responsible and how the mistake was made. Hence, they cannot take any effective actions and left with the mistake which the totality of the management made.

In retrospect, there were a few remarkable things to this episode, in spite of the probability that an ordinary person would have been put into my situation, and any person without any family to support would have carried out just what I did.

Though it was a torture for me to work in the engineering environments, possibly I knew it was necessary intuitively. I saved money and improved English and learned the engineering approach. Certainly English used in engineering is different from that used in the expository book writing for the general readers. Also engineering deals with different subjects. However, they have a great deal in common. Without the experience in engineering I could have ended up amusing myself in book writing for years and could not get the books published not realising that they did not reach acceptable standards.

It was amazing even to myself that I found myself in an ideal situation, not of my making, when I wanted to retire from the permanent job. The setup was perfect for my purpose and I could not have wished more.

When people carry out some swindle, there are always some risks involved. I tried to extract money from the government in the circumstances I happened to be in, which was possibly a form of swindle. In my case I did not have any risks of any form or shape. Incredibly there was no criminality that can be charged against me: the managers concerned did not have any prima facie criminal case against me in the court of law. Even within the government organisation, the management could not have dismissed me simply because I stopped the commissioning job which the public service acts did not specify to be my job. This was an example the government bureaucracy landed on its nose. It is a fair comment that the government department or factory of any country would make a formidable adversary, but can become vulnerable if we attack it on some weak spot. This reminds me of the story of Achilles from the Greek mythology: Though he was strong and invulnerable, he had one weak spot--his heel. He was eventually slain when wounded in the heel. I was employed in the government by the public service acts and my dismissal had to be done by the public service board which also acted as a court of law within the Federal government. Without the proof of my misconduct concerning the commissioning, which I kept to myself, the factory managers could not have taken my dismissal case to the public service board. Suppose the above board got involved in the issue from some unexplainable reasons, the management of the factory would have got into a big strife because they had to explain why the Executive

Manager ignored the promotion recommendation from one of the managers and had only some inkling of my misconduct. This was the way I assessed the circumstances with all my honesty, though some of the assessments were only the speculations, not backed by concrete evidence.

It was a most effortless task to carry on the scheme: All I did was to cease my major project, not telling anyone the reasons behind. I have noticed in the course of my life and I am sure many readers have noticed that many people cannot hold their tongue when they are under a scheme, criminal or non-criminal, and they give the game away.

I derived a great deal of satisfaction out of the perceived fury of the Executive Manager. He could not do a thing against me, and could have been blamed for the non-progress of commissioning, which added to my sense of accomplished revenge. The prime motivation of pulling the scam was to extract money from the government and at the same time I carried out the vendetta against this manager. Without the intent of retribution I would not have discontinued the project even if I had seen a chance to make substantial sum of money. My conscience was clear and I did not compromise my ethical pride through the swindle, though I was slightly hurt for the people who were anxious to see the plant commissioning complete and to use the plant for their production job.

The package was tax free at the initial payment like a lottery win and was rolled over with tax advantage, and besides the interest rate was high at the time. I calculated that if invested wisely the money would have grown to roughly a million dollars in 20 years' time when I would be 65 years of age with my savings intact. I had earlier reckoned that I would have made about a million dollars at the age of 65 if I had kept working full time and invested the savings. If we focus attention on the sequence of event, ignoring time and with some doubt on the cause and effect, I would make a million dollars by simply stopping my major project for nine months.

One word of caution. I heard many times that the person was in no-win situation: however, incredibly the circumstances of the conflict was such that I could not lose whatever happened--in no-loss situation--if this phrase exists at all. However, I learned in my life that certain things (good or bad) which I did not expect could happen. The management could have transferred me to the commissioning position, Class 2 or 3, and if I had refused to do the job, I could have been dismissed. Here again, many people in the public service pretended to do their work in order to avoid dismissal and I could have done the same. Also the above scam might not have produced the intended result unless I was firmly established in the system: the management might not have agreed to my retrenchment. Before I was transferred to the Sales Department many people expressed the opinion that I would not be transferred to another section since I was so popular as an officer-in-charge of the cap and detonator sections. I was known to be the hardest worker in the factory and also people used to call me ‘a man of the moment’. It is not hard to earn the former title: all one has to do is to work harder than anybody else around. One has to impress people every time one does a job before people call one the latter title. When a project was stuck and did not progress from various reasons, the manager in charge used to instruct the project officer to pass the job to me such that it could be finished quickly and properly. In point of fact, the commissioning job was assigned to me since it had virtually stopped progressing. I had never heard any other person who carried both of the above titles in all my life through my work and through the mass media. If there is one I like to meet that person to see what sort of personality he or she has.

The only regret I have was that I made the innocent people unhappy with the unfinished commissioning jobs. I believe that these people eventually forgave me when I told them my scheme one week before I left the government.

Lastly, in Book One under the heading of ‘Underlying Explanation of Idealism Theory: Evolution, God’s Will and Cell Theory’ I wrote a statement that provided we know precisely what happened we can write a story about an individual or a nation similar to the Bible. Section 2, Chapter 5 refers. This episode may illustrate the point. I am to attempt a biblical interpretation of the above episode in conjunction with the verse 'Sit at my right hand until I make your enemies your footstool' (Psalms 110:1). I made my enemy (Executive Manager) my footstool, which was possible only because I was single. It did not matter why I was unmarried, though that status was on me because of my belief in the Third Prophecy. Hence I can say that I won because I believed in the new philosophy. Also it is interesting to note that the above verse says 'I make' and not 'you make', indicating that God arranged everything. This was what happened in the episode: all was given to me and I merely stopped the commissioning job, sitting tight and keeping my mouth shut. The foregoing is the way I understand the Bible, though some readers may point out what I did was not in accordance with the Bible in that there were elements of scam and revenge in my intent.

Section 5 Socially

When we look at the future society as a whole where a substantial proportion of the population follow the creed of the Third Prophecy, we notice at once that most boons under 'Individually' within the present society are true at the social level as well. Certainly we have to change the expressions to suit the social perspective from the individual point of view, and also look deeper into the social implications, but we can clearly see many parallels.

I have presented largely negative pictures of the religious and communistic prophecies. I am a religious person and the religious doctrines still impress me; however, my negative opinion towards religion refers to the social impact. My main objection to religion is that they do not fully explain what we experience in our life and only partially make clear the social phenomena around us. Possibly the theories are not inherently wrong but are based on idealised pictures of the real life. Hence, people went on with their daily businesses which other factors governed, only making lip service to the principles the prominent prophets put forward. The situations were not much different in the previous communist countries and people went on the daily business, making the lip service to the ideals Karl Marx put forward.

In studying the world history, we note that some society was dominated by a group of people whose binding force was of familial, religious, economic, racial, or class nature. Nobody dispute the fact that the aggregate of these elites thus formed formulated the ruling policies in these societies. However, these policies were mostly compromises, accommodating the other various considerations. The idealistic and materialistic thoughts to which the two previous prophecies are equated, as I stress in Book One *Idealism and Materialism*, are only parts of human thoughts. Hence it is not hard for us to contemplate the circumstances where the elite went against their cherished principles, even though their power was originated in these theories. For example, the communist government often had to ignore the Marxist doctrines in implementing the policies. Also the church establishments in Europe in the medieval period at times disregarded the biblical teachings in favour of the temporal gains.

As I see, the business affairs of the world have been carried out in the main under such doctrines as 'Might is right', 'Dogs eat dogs', 'Lie and cheat' or 'Machiavellianism'. In the process, people have trampled down justice and thought it as a matter of course to live the life of injustice--sometimes as a giver and sometimes as a receiver. It was not that people did not want justice but wanted the other things in life more than justice. Often they find themselves in a position to grab an opportunity for an easy gain. People crave wealth, well-paid job, power and honour in social life and they can obtain the necessities of life, that is, food, clothes, shelter, and sex through these mediums.

Every society took the aforementioned dirty tricks for granted. When a certain ideology gripped and permeated a society, for instance, Christianity or communism, the new noble ideology did not replace but rather superimposed on those tactics. Upon introduction of the Third Prophecy in a social scale, people feel that these dirty tricks are no longer supreme. Irrespective of the type of society people live under, the new society will be gradually transformed for the better, the degree of betterment depending on, largely, what percentage of the population accept the new faith. Though the aim of the Third Prophecy does not have anything in common with the previous two prophecies, the new society shall fulfil the dreams the past thinkers cherished: idealism and materialism will come to full fruition. This notion will manifest in concrete forms in reduced population, diminished exploitation, stronger national defence, more spare time, seeking social justice and social reforms, and survival of human race, all of which lead to the fulfilment of the ideals religion and communism advocated.

In the new society most people will walk the way of virtues as taught by the ancient sages. Justice--not injustice as has been commonly practised in the past and present--will govern the society. Here, idealism shall not be the topics people merely discuss about but shall be equated with the everyday life. The ideals of materialists will also be realised in the new society. There will be abundance of food, clothes, shelter and other various consumer goods and services. The commodities will be made by advanced technology and be so cheap that most people can afford them as much as they want, which is really an ideal state of affairs the communists preached. High technology, automated production and high wages must come about to combat the scarce labour.

Once the Third Prophecy becomes widespread and many people stay single, there will be a large number of small to medium units, for sale or rent, accommodating for single people: some blocks of units are unisex and some, mixed. The units will provide, for fees, meals, cleaning and laundry services. They will cater for people when they are sick, apart from the necessary facilities to care for the elderly and disabled single people by legislation or with government assistance. There will be legitimate sexual services for men and women, which I will refer briefly in the introduction to Book Five *The Sexual Laws*. The sexual services may come under the management of the block or the government or any independent business.

In the following table I present the parallel manifestations of the Third Prophecy for the individuals and for the nations. In the succeeding pages, I am to expound the social consequences of these concepts.

Individually; at present and in the future	Socially; in the future only
a no family	a reduced population
b diminished exploitation	b diminished exploitation
c stronger personal defence	c stronger national defence
d more spare time	d more spare time
e seeking justice	e seeking social justice and social reforms
f no descendants	f survival of human race

a Reduced Population

When a large number of people don't have any children, obviously that society will have decreased population, the degree of which depending on the percentage of the population who will opt not to rear any children. I expect that the decrease in population would be sharpest in the so-called developed countries. Many scholars uphold that the overpopulation is the single greatest problem the present world is facing. I am not going to argue here if this premise is valid or not. However, I am sure that the world would have fewer problems of less seriousness, if the population becomes smaller by intelligent judgement such as the result of the general adherence to the creed of this book, rather than through other causes such as war, famine or disease. Though we should not expect that the reduced number of people on earth will solve all the social ills, it should certainly achieve the economically ideal state of affairs many economists dream. The commonly accepted view by the economists is that there must be an optimum population to a territory (Heimann 1964, p. 85). However, this view has a serious flaw in that people don't agree what the optimum population to a territory is and what criteria people use to calculate the optimum population. Also it is hard to achieve the optimum population agreed, ending up too few or most likely too many people.

The Third Prophecy does not originate in the economic considerations of the nation. Hence, the population of the nation which embraces its teaching wholeheartedly will be ever on the decrease: its people will disregard the concept of optimum population.

Karl Marx made a promise in his dreamed-up communist world that the consumer goods would be given away according to the needs of the people. It is obvious to any sensible persons that the stated aim cannot be achieved under overpopulation, and can be attained, if possible at all, when there is a sharp reduction of population from some cause as well as the high level of technology under the communist rule.

b Diminished Exploitation

The world with little exploitation in the future society under the Third Prophecy may be a corollary of diminished exploitation of individual life under any society, current or new. This conclusion naturally follows from what was discussed for the individual exploitation of the last chapter. The term 'exploitation' is used here again in its broadest sense and the absence of exploitation means prevalence of justice in any field of human activities.

As my own experience goes under the current society, justice between the feuding parties is an exception rather than a rule. I will predict with confidence that the position will be reversed in the new social system; fairness--a manifestation of justice in any transaction--will be the order of the day. The principles of exploitation presented in Section 3 of Chapter 2 in this book are meant to be universal truth and are true under any social system. However, the exploitation for the public at large in the new society has a drastically different character in the same way it has to me even in this society. People's attitude towards life then will be quite different and that fact will manifest in all human thoughts and activities. People will have higher ethical level together with higher living standard, thinking and acting accordingly.

Basically, people will feel that there is no need to lie and cheat the other human beings since they have to support only themselves who have no family of their own. Should a transgression happen, many of the transgressed individuals would not hesitate to retaliate as I did not. Some would seek legal redress which is made to punish the transgressors severely, unlike the present ineffective legal systems made by the legal fraternity ignorant of the new way of thinking. This situation is similar to the idealists ignorant of the advanced technologies trying to achieve the sophisticated effects in the field of production, medicine and defence.

c Stronger National Defence

Some critics may argue that a nation which will embrace the new philosophy enthusiastically may have a serious defence problem: this hypothetical nation of the future has a drastically reduced population with a high living standard. I can refute the above concern in a similar fashion as for the defence (or security) of the individuals who believe in and follow the Third Prophecy. It was pointed out earlier that single people, belying their bearing, were better placed in the struggles for existence than married people with children. By the similar reasoning, I believe that the new society will be stronger than the other comparable societies with the old beliefs.

In the new society:

- People will have higher moral standards than in the former society. Exploitation will be minimised. Justice will be widespread and many people will not tolerate injustice in any form.
- There will be advanced knowledge in many fields, which will be applied to develop the sophisticated defence system. A large number of people with spare time will devote their time for the advancement of science and technology.
- At the war emergency, many people who normally work part time will work full time for the national service and home front.

For the reasons cited above, the nation which incorporates the Third Prophecy to its heart will be the strongest among the nations comparable in land mass and resources. The number of defence personnel deployed is large for the population and they will be well trained and supplied with various kinds of high-tech equipment. The defence forces will have, per defence personnel, a large number of aircrafts, warships and ground vehicles, with various precision rockets all of which are made to the state of the art quality. The forces as a whole are highly mechanised but some units are trained to face scattered insurgents.

d More Spare Time

I point out in Book One *Idealism and Materialism* that spare time is one of the causes of a civilisation. Section 1 of Chapter 7 refers.

It is hard to predict with certainty what people, men and women, will do if they are freed from supporting the family. However, the following assessments sound fair to me:

- Some people will use all their time and energy to try to accumulate what they desire such as wealth and power.
- Some people will keep working and seek after the pleasures of life. For example, they go on frequent pleasure trips, or indulge in gambling or drinking.
- Some people will become inactive and loaf their days, not engaging in the permanent employment.

However, I am hoping that many people with so much spare time will not follow any of the above courses of actions, but will spend their time in the fashion the ancient to classical Greeks thought to be ideal. As a matter of fact, I took this line and chose to do what I like most in my life, that is, reading and writing.

The ancient to classical Greeks in their golden age shunned labour and believed it ideal to devote their time and energy to creative works such as drama, literature and politics. In contrast, the modern civilised people prefer to spend spare time on various leisure activities, since most people today, even successful, must commit their major time to earn a living for themselves and their families.

Most of the free Greeks then had considerable assets including a few slaves of Greeks and non-Greeks, all of which made the above proposition possible. Women, slaves and foreigners were excluded from the social activities on the premise that only the free Greek men were capable of meaningfully engaging in the creative and social activities. We can see that this premise, racism and sexism in the current phrase, made possible both the spare time for the free Greek men and the flowering of the Greek civilisation. Since women, slaves and non-Greeks are known to have constituted the bulk of the population in Athens, a representative Greek city in the ancient to classical prosperity, the political system adopted there was anything but democratic in the modern sense of the term: it was democratic only among the free Greek males. Here we can see the contradiction of the ancient to classical Greek world: though they achieved magnificent culture, one of the highest achieved by human race, it stood on racism and sexism. I believe that this is the seed of decline sown at the time of origination. Engels wrote that the real cause of the fall of the Athenian state was its slavery, bringing the labour of the free citizens into contempt (Marx & Engels 1970, p. 284). The ancient to classical Greek society was just and fair among the free Greek men, but women and the non-Greek males which formed the bulk of the population were sacrificed. Accordingly I can say the ancient to classical Greek community as a whole did not practise the concept of 'Love thy neighbour', the kernel of idealism.

In the ancient to classical Greek world, the Greeks took it for granted to build superior culture sacrificing women and non-Greeks. Most of the slaves were non-Greeks and the insignificant opposition to the slavery came mainly from the small number of the Greeks that the Greeks should not be slaves. When Hitler wanted to do the same by sacrificing non-Aryans and women, he faced the furious oppositions from all over the world. Today's general opinion is to praise the ancient to classical Greeks and denigrate Hitler. This is not really fair, though certainly there are other considerations we have to take into account other than racism and sexism in the assessments.

In the modern advanced countries of the world the spare time has been created by machines which were made by accumulated technologies. Majority of people still must engage in the full-time occupations to make a decent living and their spare time is much less than the ancient to classical Greeks had.

In the society under the sway of the Third Prophecy, the spare time will not be generated by the property which included slaves as was done in the ancient to classical Greek society, but will be created by non-commitment to the family life together with advanced knowledge, especially in technology and industry. The ancient to classical Greeks had to sacrifice a large number of people to achieve the desired status but in the new society I am proposing, people do not have to expend a group of people to have spare time. As a rule of thumb, 40 hours a week is the normal working hours in the economically advanced countries today. I would reckon that for the individuals who don't have a family, 20 hours a week is more than enough to maintain the same standard of living today and in the future. Further, the single people do not have the family to look after. This simple assessment of single men and married men are not valid if their wives work and they do not have children.

Thus, in the new society, I hope that people will spend enormous time learning about idealism, materialism and the various arts. I would imagine that the rapid progress in science and technology we are currently experiencing will not slow down in the society where the Third Prophecy is in full bloom, even with drastically diminished population, nay, the progress will be accelerated heaps and bounds. Scarce labour will force the developments of science and technologies, automation of production and high wages of the employed. However, idealism is a completed entity and it is not possible to further advance it in any drastic degree. All people can do concerning idealism is to learn and research the past literature which was all but completed at the early classical era. People can only learn and practise established idealism. The various arts such as painting, poetry, music, sculpture and literature will be further developed by the people who are interested in them. However, I have some reservation as I have about idealism, if these arts will exceed what was achieved in the past. It is certain, though, that they will be enhanced in the modern settings to suit the modern people.

<u>e Seeking Social Justice and Social Reforms</u>

I don't think I am exaggerating when I say majority of attempts to remedy social ills have been in vain in the long course of human history. In fact this assessment is obvious from the viewpoint of the Third Prophecy. We should not expect that the people who are not acquainted with this new philosophy to allow effective corrective measures: these people do not know how to love their own children and further are busy looking after the fruits of their desire. I dare say only when a substantial number of people believe in and practise the doctrine of the Third Prophecy can we expect all well-conceived reforms to be effective and lasting, and it cannot be otherwise. Only when human beings are in the last stage of evolution, will we find that any good reforms are meaningful and have a fair chance of success, since we are dealing with people who are capable of standing on their feet not relying on the family.

In the new society the people who keep having children become the minority, of not necessarily the numerical sense, and the believers of the Third Prophecy dominate the society taking the leads in effecting the social justice. The division of labour will exist between the two groups of people. Hence even if we uphold that the former is morally inferior and carry on the business of the population maintenance, still the latter will carry out the social reforms effectively.

f Survival of Human Race

The members of the public have shown a huge upsurge of concern over the environmental issues in recent years, as a result of the reported degradations, which in turn resulted from production and consumption of huge number of commodities for the large population. It is often alleged that the degradation of our surrounding world is one of the most serious threats to human existence. The fact that I don't have any children makes me feel the environmental problems of any sort are irrelevant to me. I also believe that any other person with no child of their blood would feel the same way. However, the cursory analyses reveal that I have done more for the environment than most of the vocal environmentalists. For Karl Marx and his contemporary educated people, the production was the focus of attention and the consumption was the subsidiary idea. The depletion of the natural resources and environmental degradations did not worry them, either. Capitalism was in its infancy at the time and these problems simply did not exist, or so they thought.

I don't have any family so I have to pay heavy tax on my income. The tax thus collected is used to alleviate the problems people are complaining about. In this respect the tax collection of today is not user pay and is not really fair since the people who create the least problems are the ones who are burdened most. People with a large family should pay more tax as a penalty of degrading the environment.

To start with, having no children results in less use of resources and hence less pollution in a most effective way. I have never heard the environmentally conscious people try to tackle the problems from the viewpoint of reduced population, probably because they may be married with a few children, whose fact made them think about environments in the first place. Marriage and children have been sacred cow throughout human history and people's right to both has never been questioned. Even the slaves in the antique society were generally encouraged to procreate, if not to marry, since the more slaves meant the more wealth for the owners in the same token that the more cattle meant the more wealth.

I would say that the Third Prophecy would be the most powerful weapon people can think of to combat the depletion of natural resources and the environmental damages. Interestingly, though, the believers of this philosophy will not have any interest in the environment since they don't have any descendants to be worried about and their utmost concern is the love of their children as I define. To solve the environmental problems in the most effective way is only one of the minor by-products of the Third Prophecy.

The human race needs widespread practice of the Third Prophecy for its survival. It will perish without the new way of thinking and subsequent actions by a large number of the world population as I outline in this book. This may sound paradoxical without going into depths of the matter since this philosophy teaches people not to have a child. How many times do I go through this dilemma from the various viewpoints, the humans cannot survive unless an entirely new philosophy such as described in this book is introduced into this world.

According to historic literature, the ancient people generally believed a large number of children were a symbol of success and wealth apart from being the source of joys. The idea was assisted by the incredibly high mortality rate compared with today's standard. Many of them strove to have as many children as they could, irrespective of economic consequences of personal and social dimensions. The ancients looked at the world as infinite and with fear--the fear of the unknown as well as the possible enemies (humans and animals) around. One way of overcoming the fear was to create as many children as possible and the infinite world outlook nurtured the idea. One of the cardinal promises of the Old Testament was that the Israelites would have a vast number of descendants like the sands of the sea shore or the stars in the heaven, if they followed the precepts of God. In the modern civilised societies the above concept is not in general regarded in high esteem and the birth control is widely practised. However, even today among the underdeveloped nations, people look on a large number of children as something desirable and tend to have as many children as they can afford. Apart from looking at children as status symbol or source of happiness, people in the poorest countries of today's world often see their offspring as a source of practical importance. They look at children as labour source. Also they make as many children as they can in order to see how many of them will survive: the surviving offspring will hopefully support them when they get old and can no longer support themselves. Unlike the developed nations, the undeveloped nations do not have the welfare system in place to look after the aged and incapacitated.

Even the unicellular organisms, the simplest form of life, such as amoeba, are ever striving to multiply their offspring by cell divisions. If the surrounding world is favourable for their living, they multiply their kinds enormously. If totally unsuited, they perish without a trace.

Charles Darwin in his famous book *On the Origin of Species* (1859) narrates how the animals and plants strive to survive and to increase their kinds using all their tricks and intelligence available. By careful observations, he discovered that every piece on earth is, in reality, a theatre of competition by the living things. The fittest animals or plants for the particular patch of land survive and multiply, mostly sacrificing other species on the way and occasionally cooperating with others if that suits their existence. He also argues that the death struggles for existence gives rise to the evolution of the diverse species to adapt and change to the environments--weather and various physical makeups of the surround--they happen to be in. The evolution is biological changes, and not cultural changes which took place in the historical development of the humans. Thus the huge varieties of animals and plants we observe today have resulted from the strong and innate desire to survive and multiply, which is the fundamental drive of all living things.

The human race has behaved similarly as the other living things have throughout the human existence on earth, individually and as a group. A small number of people in the past might have wished a smaller population for whatever reasons; however, they were an insignificant minority and the bulk of the population decided the issue to the contrary. The world population has ever increased excepting for checks from explainable reasons, such as wars, diseases, widespread crop failures or simply lack of food.

If the world population increases at the present level, however rapid the progress of science and technology may be, we will not be able to ensure a comfortable life for most of the people on earth. This is where the Third Prophecy comes into play, though its inception does not have anything to do with the considerations of economics and population. The reduced population is only an incidental and possibly insignificant consequence of the prophecy.

Some economists would argue that the reduced population does not necessarily lead to a higher standard of living in a region. Some densely populated countries enjoy economically good living and some sparsely populated countries have low levels of incomes. This argument may be true; however, we cannot dispute the following observations:

- A large population of a region reduces land and the natural resources per capita, that is, an individual will have less land, mineral resources, fish, timber and so on, by apportionment.
- A large population increases pollution and damages environment. It has been definitely true up to the present anyway that the population increase outstripped technical competence and the capital expenditures to contain the environmental damages. Some people may argue for

the huge capital expenditure on technical innovations to prevent the environmental degradation; however, they strongly go against what has been established so far, and also go against one assertion of the Third Prophecy, that is, the people before the spread of this philosophy are morally inferior.
- The overpopulation of a nation has been always conducive to the desire to make war. The effort to contain wars by the good government policies and the cooperation among the nations, to my judgement, has been insignificant and futile in the face of the serious and overwhelming tide of overpopulation; in fact it was a lot easier to solve the problem by wars.

It is reported through the media in the recent years that some rivers, some lakes and even some parts of the sea are dying: they are devoid of fish, aquatic plants and animals. The scientists have measured that the sea level rose as much as 10-20 cm in the last one hundred years, and these scientists predict it will rise another one metre in the next one hundred years. They theorised the figures based on the notion that the global warming melts the polar ice above the sea level, thus raising the sea level itself. Scientists who studied the temperature records of over the past 100 years concluded a rise in global temperature of about 0.5 degree centigrade. It is also scientifically predicted that the air temperature of the globe may increase on average two degrees in the next 50 years.

The records of atmospheric temperatures were kept as early as the 17th century; however, it was not until about 1850 when the well calibrated instruments were used that we can use them for statistical purpose.

The burning of fossil fuels (coal, oil and natural gas) produces carbon dioxide. The amount of carbon dioxide in the atmosphere has increased more than 10% in the last 30 years, which is said to be the results of the burning of fossil fuels as well as the destruction of forests. Chief among the greenhouse gases which trap the heat in the atmosphere is carbon dioxide, which raise the global temperature. Most of the burning takes place in automobiles, electric power plants and manufacturing facilities. Trees remove carbon dioxide from the atmosphere by the process called photosynthesis, hence deforestation means less removal of carbon dioxide from the environment.

Though global warming has beneficial effects such as allowing farming in the area where the cold climate prevented in the past, most effects are adverse altering the ecology of the globe as a whole. The global warming changes the rainfall patterns, melts enough polar ice to raise the sea level, increases the severity of tropical storms and changes the habitat of the plants and animals.

The man-made chemical chlorofluorocarbons have created holes in the stratospheric ozone layers, particularly over Antarctica. A growing depletion of the ozone layer over temperate climate where a large number of people live was recently discovered. The ozone layer serves as a shield against ultraviolet radiation which causes skin cancer.

Undoubtedly the degradation of aquatic environment has been going on for quite some time. Even if we make allowance for the increased environmental awareness of the general public and also for the more accurate assessment techniques available at present, people are appalled with the high degree of damages to the aquatic environments. The unrestricted population growth or restricted only by war, pestilence and famine had in the past the fatal flaw in that it brought suffering to many people and destroyed what had been constructed. Malthus thought that people paid the penalty of being stupid and the government should not interfere with the process.

As more precise measurements and diverse studies were carried out, scientists recently issued more and more dire predictions about the environment. It seems that scientists are firming on the opinion that the major cause of the global warming was man-made rather than natural phenomenon such as the change of weather pattern. Dr Pep Canadell, the executive director of the Global Carbon Project, says that the world will be hotter by 4 to 6 degrees by the end of the 21st century if we do not take drastic actions. One serious problem in the past was that scientists underestimated the vast amount of methane and carbon dioxide the permafrost in the Polar Regions contained. The melting of the permafrost will release these chemicals, which drastically accelerate the ongoing damages done by the world population.

To curb the population growth is a must for the world not only for comfortable life for the majority of people but also for evading an unexpected catastrophe as a result of the licentious environmental damages. I am inclined to believe that the disaster that may overtake the world is not the kinds predicted by scientists such as global warming, degradation of the environment and depletion of the stratospheric ozone layers, but of the kind nobody has ever mentioned, because that was the scenario of misfortune that overtook me when I had kept sinning--a scenario of sudden and unforeseen catastrophe.

I would further state that the reduced population is the only avenue possible for sheer survival of human race. Thus, the Third Prophecy is correct even when we view in relation to the continuation of decent human livings, since some people will reject the prophecy and the human life on earth will be carried on happily or unhappily, depending on how people judge.

Reference List with Text Citations Marked

Bradley, John 1988, *The Russian Revolution,* Bison Books, London.
93

Burguiere, A; Klapisch-Zuber, C; Segalen, M & Zonabend, F (eds) 1996, *A History of the Family,* vol. 1, Polity Press, Cambridge.
24 (24) (24) (24) 24 (24) (24) (24) (24) (24) (24) (25)

Burnett, Dr Rosalie 1990, *Human Behavior,* The Marshall Cavendish Encyclopedia of Personal Relationships, vol. 7, Marshall Cavendish, New York.
5

Chan, Wing-Tsit (trans. and comp.) 1963, *A Source Book in Chinese Philosophy,* Princeton University Press, Princeton.
59 (59) (60)

Chien, Szuma 1979, *Selections from Records of the Historian,* trans Yang Hsien-yi and Gladys Yang, Foreign Languages Press, Peking.
38

Cotterell, Arthur (ed.) 1993, *The Penguin Encyclopedia of Classical Civilizations,* Penguin Group, Hong Kong.
6

Cotterell, Arthur & Morgan, David 1975, *China: An Integrated Study,* Harrap, London.
67 71 72

Davison, Michael Worth (ed.) 1993, *When, Where, Why and How It Happened,* Reader's Digest, London.
74 74

Dye, Howard S; Moore, John R & Holly, J Fred 1966, *Economics: Principles, Problems and Perspectives,* Allyn and Bacon Inc, Boston.
54

Ebrey, Patricia Buckley 1996, *The Cambridge Illustrated History of China,* Calmann & King Ltd, London.
63 (64) 72 74 74 (74) (74) 75 77

Eliade, Mircea 1978, *From the Stone Age to the Eleusinian Mysteries,* A History of Religious Ideas, vol. 1, trans. Willard R Trask, University of Chicago Press, Chicago.
3 (3) 57

-----1982, *From Gautama Buddha to the Triumph of Christianity,* A History of Religious Ideas, vol. 2, trans. Willard R Trask, University of Chicago Press, Chicago.
59

Freeman, Charles 1996, *Egypt, Greece and Rome: Civilizations of the Ancient Mediterranean,* Oxford University Press, New York.
5 25

Freud, Sigmund 1982, *The Interpretation of Dreams,* trans. and ed. James Strachey, George Allen & Unwin Ltd, London.
40 (40) (40) (41) (41) (41) (41) (41) (41) (41) (41) (41) (41) (41) (41) (41)

Fryer, Jonathan 1975, *The Great Wall of China,* New English Library, London.
39

Grant, Michael 1969, *The Ancient Mediterranean,* Trinity Press, London.
97

Grenville, JAS 1994, *The Collins History of the World in the Twentieth Century,* HarperCollins, London.
48 61 74 (74)

Guisso, RWL & Pagani, C 1989, *The First Emperor of China,* ed. D Miller, Sidgwick & Jackson, London.
38 (38) (38) (38) 39 68

Guntrip, Harry 1964, *Healing the Sick Mind,* George Allen & Unwin Ltd, London.
40 (40) (40) 41 42 (42) (42) (42) (42) (42) (42) 43

Guthrie, WKC 1969, *A History of Greek Philosophy,* vol. 3, Cambridge University Press, Cambridge.
34

Harbottle, Thomas Benfield 1897, *Dictionary of Quotations (Classical) or Classical Quotations, Swan* Sonnenschein & Co Ltd, London.
3 (3) (3) (3) (3) (3) 6 20 28 (28) (28) (28) 28 (29) (29) (29) 100 (100) (101) (101) (101) (101) (101)

Harris, Nathaniel 1999, *Hamlyn History of Imperial China,* Octopus Publishing Group Limited, London.
58 (59) 63 (63) 74

Heimann, Eduard 1964, *History of Economic Doctrines,* Oxford University Press, New York.
79 116

Hitler, A 1992, *Mein Kampf,* trans. Ralph Manheim, Pimlico, London.
65

Hutchins, Robert Maynard (ed.) 1952, *The Prince by Nicole Machiavelli; Leviathan by Thomas Hobbes,* Great Books of the Western World, vol. 23, Encyclopaedia Britannica Series, William Benton, Chicago.
83 97

Janaway, Christopher 1994, *Schopenhauer,* Oxford University Press, Oxford.
14 (14) (14)

Janus, Samuel S & Janus, Cynthia L 1994, *The Janus Report on Sexual Behavior,* John Wiley & Sons Inc, New York.
5 (5) (5)

Koller, John M 1985, *Oriental Philosophies,* 2nd edn, Charles Scribner's Sons, New York.
73

Lloyd, Charles W (ed.) 1964, *Human Reproduction and Sexual Behavior,* Lea & Febiger, Philadelphia.
24 25

Loewe, Michael 1990, *The Pride That Was China,* Sidgwick and Jackson, London.
68 77

Lopez, DS Jr 1987, *A Study of Svatantrika,* Snow Lion Publications, Ithaca, New York.
17

Lopez, Donald S Jr (ed.) 1996, *Religions of China in Practice,* Princeton University Press, Princeton.
59 71

McGreal, Ian P (ed.) 1995, *Great Thinkers of the Eastern World,* Harper Collins Publishers Inc, New York.
32

McTaggart, Douglas; Findley, Christopher & Parkin, Michael 1992, *Economics,* Addison-Wesley Publishing Co, Sydney.
61 83

Malthus, TR 1970, *An Essay on the Principle of Population and a Summary View of the Principle of Population,* ed. Antony Flew, Penguin books series, Hazell Watson & Viney Ltd, Aylesbury, Great Britain.
30 50 (50) (50) (50) (50) (51) (51) (51) (51) (51) (51) (51) (51) (51) (51) (52) 52 (52) (53) (53) (53) (53) (53) (53) (53)

Marx, Karl 1959, *Capital,* vol. III: *The Process of Capitalist Production as a Whole,* trans. and ed. Frederick Engels, Progress publishers, Moscow.
62

-----1963, *Theories of Surplus Value,* part I, (Capital, vol. IV), trans. Emile Burns and ed. S Ryazanskaya, Progress Publishers, Moscow.
62

-----1968, *Theories of Surplus Value,* part II, (Capital, vol. IV), trans. and ed. S Ryazanskaya, Progress Publishers, Moscow.
61 62

Marx, Karl & Engels, Frederick 1970, *Selected Works,* vol. 3, Progress Publishers, Moscow.
80 118

-----1989, *Selected Works,* revised edn, vol. 1, Progress Publishers, Moscow.
80

Mathers, Powys (trans.) 1953, *The Thousand Nights and One Night,* vol. 2, Routledge & Kegan Paul Ltd, London.
4

Mathias, P 1969, *The First Industrial Nation: An Economic History of Britain 1700-1914,* Methuen & Co Ltd, London.
32 65

Mercer, Derrik (editor-in-chief) 1996, *Chronicle of the World,* Dorling Kindersley, London.
29 (30) (30)

Milston, Gwendda 1978, *A Short History of China,* Cassell Australia, Stanmore, NSW.
62

Montaigne, Michel de 1965, *The Complete Essays of Montaigne,* trans. DM Frame, Stanford University Press, California.
2 (2) (2) (2) 15 28 29 35 (35) (36) 37 41

Murowchick, Robert E (ed.) 1994, *China: Ancient Culture, Modern Land,* Cradles of Civilization Series, Weldon Russell Pty Ltd, North Sydney.
64 75

Narada, Thera (trans.) 1993, *The Dhammapada,* 4th edn, Buddhist Council of NSW Inc, Eastlakes, NSW.
16 47

North, Sir Thomas (trans.) 1967, *North's Plutarch,* 6 vols, AMS Press Inc, New York.
7

Oliphant, Margaret 1992, *The Atlas of the Ancient World,* Random House Australia, Milsons Point, NSW.
38 56

Pushkin, Alexander 1995, *Eugene Onegin,* A Novel in Verse, trans. James E Falen, Oxford University Press, Oxford.
49 (49) (49) (49)

Randall, John Herman Jr 1976, *The Making of the Modern Mind,* Columbia University Press, New York.
13

Robbins, Lionel 1998, *A History of Economic Thought,* Princeton University Press, Princeton.
50 79

Roberts, JAG 1998, *Modern China: An Illustrated History,* Sutton Publishing Limited, Gloucester, Britain.
71 (71) (71) (71) (71) (71) 72 (72) (72)

Rousseau, JJ 1979, *Reveries of the Solitary Walker,* trans. Peter France, Penguin Books Ltd, Harmondsworth, Middlesex.
Reproduced by permission of Penguin Books Ltd.
11 (12) (12) (12) (12) 13

Rowse, AL 1979, *The Story of Britain,* Artus Publishing Co Ltd, London.
13

Schopenhaur, Arthur 1962, *The Essential Schopenhaur,* George Allen & Unwin Ltd, London.
29 (29) (29) (29)

Shakespeare, William 1985, *Hamlet, Prince of Denmark,* ed. Philip Edwards, Cambridge University Press, Cambridge.
8

Sharma, Arvind (ed.) 1993, *Our Religions,* Harper, San Francisco.
59

Smith, Adam 1991, *Wealth of Nations,* Great Minds Series, Prometheus Books, Buffalo, New York.
54

Smith, Anthony 1968, *The Body,* Unwin Brothers Ltd, London.
27

Spielvogel, Jackson J 1991, *Western Civilization,* West Publishing Co, St Paul.
61 64 70 75

Stryk, Lucien (ed.) 1982, *World of the Buddha: An Introduction to Buddhist Literature,* Grove Press Inc, New York.
4

Thomas A Kempis 1952, *The Imitation of Christ,* Penguin Classics, trans. Leo Sherley-Price, Penguin Books, Middlesex, England.
13 (13)

Toynbee, AJ 1962, *A Study of History,* abridged by DC Somervell, Oxford University Press, London.
38

Toynbee, A; Mant, AK; Smart, N; Hinton, J; Yudkin, S; Rhode, E; Heywood, R & Price, HH 1968, *Man's Concern with Death,* Hodder and Stoughton, London.
3

Velde, Van de 1965, *Ideal Marriage,* 2nd edn, Greenwood Press, Westport, Connecticut.
26 (26) (26) (26)

Walker, A 1978, *Marx: His Theory and Its Context,* Longman, London.
12

Ward, K (ed.) 1989, *Great Disasters,* Reader's Digest Association Inc, New York.
54 72 (73) (73)

Wells, HG 1925, *The Outline of History,* revised edn, 2 vols, Cassell and Co Ltd, London.
12

Westheimer, Dr Ruth 1994, *Encyclopaedia of Sex,* Element Books, Brisbane, Queensland.
40

Whitehouse, Ruth & Wilkins, John 1986, *The Making of Civilization: History Discovered through Archaeology,* Collins, London.
32 57

Index

www.ingramcontent.com/pod-product-compliance
Lightning Source LLC
LaVergne TN
LVHW081150110826
845149LV00008B/1611

* 9 7 8 0 9 9 2 3 2 9 7 7 8 *